ideas

ideas

+lighting
+iluminación
+éclairage
+beleuchtung

AUTHORS
Fernando de Haro & Omar Fuentes

EDITORIAL DESIGN & PRODUCTION

PROJECT MANAGERS
Edali Nuñez Daniel
Laura Mijares Castellá

COORDINATION
Laura Mar Hernández Morales

PREPRESS COORDINATION
Carolina Medina Granados

COPYWRITER
Roxana Villalobos

ENGLISH TRANSLATION
Babel International Translators

FRENCH TRANSLATION
Architextos: Translation Services and Language Solutions

GERMAN TRANSLATION
Angloamericano de Cuernavaca
Sabine Klein

Ideas
+lighting . +iluminación . +éclairage . +beleuchtung

© 2011, Fernando de Haro & Omar Fuentes

AM Editores S.A. de C.V.
Paseo de Tamarindos 400 B, suite 109, Col. Bosques de las Lomas,
C.P. 05120, México, D.F., Tel. 52(55) 5258 0279
E-mail: ame@ameditores.com   www.ameditores.com

ISBN: 978-607-437-088-1

Printed in China.

introduction   introducción

It goes without saying that the best results in a home can only ever be achieved by carefully balancing architecture, decoration and lighting.

Good lighting of indoor and outdoor spaces in a home requires the right combination of two factors: the functional aspect by which a place or object is illuminated in order to provide adequate visibility; and decorative considerations regarding the esthetic usage of light in a given space.

Es posible afirmar que para llegar a resultados óptimos en una casa, su arquitectura, decoración e iluminación deben interrelacionarse.

La buena iluminación de los espacios interiores y exteriores de una casa depende de saber combinar dos factores: uno funcional, destinado a dotar un lugar u objeto de luz para que ofrezca una visibilidad confortable, y otro decorativo, que se refiere a la representación estética de la luz en el espacio.

introduction   einleitung

Pour réussir au mieux sa maison, il n'est pas exagéré d'affirmer que l'architecture, la décoration et l'éclairage doivent pouvoir interagir dans un même but.

Un bon éclairage des espaces intérieurs et extérieurs d'une demeure repose sur une conjugaison réussie entre deux facteurs. Le premier est fonctionnel : il est nécessaire qu'un lieu, que des objets, soient éclairés pour être suffisamment visibles. L'autre est décoratif : on parle ici des caractéristiques esthétiques de la lumière dans l'espace.

Es ist unumgänglich die Architektur, Dekoration und Beleuchtung eines Hauses miteinander abzustimmen, um ein Haus optimal einzurichten.

Eine gute Beleuchtung in den Innen- und Aussenbereichen eines Hauses hängt davon ab, wie man zwei Faktoren zu kombinieren versteht; den Funktionellen, der den Bereich mit einem eine angenehmen Sicht erlaubenden Licht ausstattet und den Dekorativen, der sich auf die ästhetische Rolle des Lichts im Raum bezieht.

Getting the lighting just right in a defined context is an undertaking that requires close examination of each specific place. This includes the crucial task of considering how each room in the home is oriented, as well as the type and amount of daylight that enters each area at different times of the day and over the different seasons of the year. Just as important is planning artificial light and identifying the kind of atmosphere required for each place, bearing in mind the activities to be carried out there.

This volume explores four basic types of lighting that can bring out the full splendor of a setting: decorative, accent, indirect and daylight. With this classification very much in mind, the book has been subdivided into specific areas inside the house – living room, dining room, bathroom and bedroom – along with the outdoor area, including the terrace.

The pages of this book set out solutions that have been put to the test by experts, as well as techniques

Conseguir la iluminación deseada en un contexto es una tarea que demanda la observación de cada sitio en específico. En este análisis es primordial considerar la orientación que tiene cada habitación en la vivienda, la calidad y cantidad de luz natural que penetra en las distintas áreas, durante las diversas estaciones del año y a diferentes horas del día. Simultáneamente es necesario realizar la planificación de la luz eléctrica y aclarar cuál es la atmósfera que se desea conseguir en cada lugar, tomando en cuenta las tareas que se llevan a cabo en él.

Para este volumen se han clasificado cuatro tipos básicos de iluminación con los que se puede llegar a conquistar un ambiente agradable: decorativa, de acento, indirecta y natural. Tomando en consideración estas tipologías, a su vez el libro se ha subdividido en algunos espacios interiores de la casa –sala, comedor, baño y recámara–, dejando una parte a exteriores, incluyendo la terraza.

Obtenir l'éclairage voulu dans un lieu particulier est une tâche qui nécessite une bonne observation spécifique de chaque pièce. Au cours de cette analyse, il est indispensable de réfléchir à l'orientation de chacune des pièces de la demeure ainsi qu'à la quantité et à la qualité de lumière naturelle qui y pénètre au cours de la journée mais aussi au fil des saisons. Il est en outre nécessaire d'élaborer le projet de l'installation électrique et de choisir clairement quelle atmosphère on souhaite créer pour chaque espace sans oublier quelles activités s'y dérouleront en général.

Cet ouvrage aborde quatre types d'éclairage basique grâce auxquels on peut obtenir une atmosphère agréable : décoratif, ponctuel (accentué), indirect et naturel. Ce livre suit donc cette classification mais il est divisé en fonction des pièces de la maison : salon, salle à manger, salle de bain, chambre. L'ouvrage se termine par les espaces extérieurs comme la terrasse.

Die gewünschte Beleuchtung für einen Raum zu finden, ist eine Aufgabe, die die Beobachtung jedes eines Platzes erfordert. Bei dieser Analyse ist es grundlegend zu bedenken, wie die Räume im Haus ausgerichtet sind und wie die Qualität und die Intensität des natürlichen Lichtes beschaffen ist, das im Verlauf der Jahreszeiten und während verschiedener Tageszeiten auf bestimmte Bereiche fällt. Gleichzeitig ist es notwendig, den Einsatz von künstlichem Licht zu planen und zu klären, welche Atmosphäre man in den einzelnen Bereichen erreichen möchte, wobei man die Aufgaben berücksichtigen sollte, die in ihnen ausgeführt werden.

Für diesen Band wurde das Thema Beleuchtung in vier Grundtypen unterteilt, mit denen man ein angenehmes Ambiente schaffen kann: dekoratives, akzentuierendes, indirektes und natürliches Licht. Diese Einteilung berücksichtigend, wurde das Buch wiederum in einzelne Bereiche des Hauses – Wohnzimmer, Esszimmer, Badezimmer und

for using light to create sensations of extensiveness or greater height; or how to infuse a setting with warmth or coldness by harnessing the color of lights. There are also some useful tips on how to select the right amount of light, its tone, how to direct it and the best way to achieve one impression or another, along with guidelines on when it is a good idea to use accents or what to do to increase or tone down luminosity, to mention but a few of the numerous possibilities covered.

Lighting is an integral project which is why all the different components involved need to be taken into account: loose lights, rails, types of lights, potency, the glints and glimmers they produce, the characteristics of the surfaces they are shone onto and how they reflect light, intensity variables that can be obtained, the use of candles or a fireplace in a given moment, etc.

Lastly, we hope readers will find this book useful, but we also strongly recommend energy-saving bulbs that will allow users to save money while, at the same time, helping protect the environment.

A lo largo de las páginas se presentan soluciones que han sido probadas por los expertos, así como algunos trucos que muestran cómo a través de la iluminación se gana la sensación de amplitud o de mayor altura; o cómo desarrollar la emoción de calidez o frialdad de un ambiente a partir del color de las luminarias. También hay consejos útiles que ayudan a escoger la cantidad de luz, el tono de ésta, la manera de direccionarla y la forma en la que se tiene que difundir para alcanzar tal o cual impresión; o bien que señalan en qué casos es pertinente incluir un acento y cómo hacerlo, o qué hacer para disminuir o incrementar la luminosidad, entre muchas otras posibilidades.

Como queda implícito, un proyecto de iluminación es integral y por ello es necesario tener en cuenta todos los elementos lumínicos en juego: luces sueltas, rieles, tipos de lámparas, potencias, los brillos y destellos que emiten, las características de las superficies sobre las que son direccionadas y el modo en que éstas reflejan la luz, las variables de intensidad que se pueden conseguir, la presencia de velas o del fuego de la chimenea en un momento dado…

Por último, además de desear al lector que este libro le sea de utilidad, vale la pena recomendar el uso de luminarias ahorradoras de energía, pues éstas no solamente son redituables para el consumo, sino también más amigables con el medio ambiente.

Page après page, de nombreuses solutions avalisées par des experts sont reproduites ainsi que quelques astuces qui montrent que l'on peut agrandir une pièce et la doter d'une atmosphère chaude ou froide en jouant simplement sur la lumière ou sur les couleurs des luminaires. D'autres conseils sont également prodigués pour bien choisir la quantité de lumière adéquate, pour la diriger convenablement, pour sélectionner ses couleurs, pour parvenir à telle ou telle ambiance et pour augmenter ou diminuer la luminosité. Le livre montre, de plus, dans quelles circonstances un éclairage ponctuel est conseillé et comment y parvenir.

Il va sans dire que l'on doit tenir compte de nombreux facteurs lorsque l'on prévoit l'éclairage d'une demeure. On doit ainsi choisir à l'avance avec précision son type de luminaire : lampes à une seule ampoule ou à plusieurs (rail luminaire par exemple), types de lampes (forme, intensité), éclat des ampoules, particularités des superficies éclairées par une lumière ponctuelle, façon dont la lumière est reflétée, intensité que l'on peut régler, rôle joué par les bougies ou la cheminée à tel ou tel moment si c'est le cas …

Les auteurs de ce livre espèrent donc que cet ouvrage sera très utile aux lecteurs et terminent cette introduction avec un dernier conseil : celui d'utiliser des ampoules à économie d'énergie qui ne permettent pas simplement de limiter ses dépenses mais de contribuer également à la protection de l'environnement.

Schlafzimmer-, unterteilt, einen weiteren Teil den Aussenbereichen, einschliesslich der Terrasse, widmend.

Im Verlauf des Buches werden von Fachleuten erprobte Lösungen vorgestellt, so wie einige Tricks, die zeigen, wie man durch die Beleuchtung den Eindruck von Weite oder grösserer Höhe gewinnen kann; oder wie man den Eindruck von Wärme oder Kühle durch den Farbton der Beleuchtung entstehen lässt. Es sind auch nützliche Ratschläge zu finden, die helfen, die Stärke der Beleuchtung, deren Farbton, wie sie auszurichten ist und die Form der Ausbreitung des Lichts, um den einen oder anderen Eindruck zu erreichen, zu wählen; oder auch in welchem Fall es angebracht ist, etwas zu betonen und wie man das macht, oder wie man Helligkeit verstärkt oder vermindert, um nur einige der vielen Möglichkeiten zu nennen.

Wie daraus hervorgeht, umfasst die Planung der Beleuchtung viele Aspekte und darum sollten alle zur Verfügung stehenden Beleuchtungsarten in Betracht gezogen werden: einzelne Lampen, Lichtleisten, verschiedene Lampenarten, Lichtstärke, durch sie verursachte Reflektionen, die Reflektionseigenschaften der Oberflächen, auf die sie gerichtet sind, die Bandbreite möglicher Intensität, die Präsenz von Kerzen oder Kaminfeuer in bestimmten Momenten ...

Zum Abschluss, zusätzlich zu dem Wunsch, dass dieses Buch dem Leser von Nutzen ist, ist die Verwendung von Energiesparlampen zu empfehlen, da diese beim Verbrauch sparen und damit umweltfreundlicher sind.

living rooms
salas
salons
wohnzimmer

decorative light
luz decorativa
éclairage décoratif
dekoratives licht

The living room is a place that needs to look good, so planning the lighting scheme carefully, including the vital contribution of decorative lighting, is of paramount importance. Lights with translucent screens that emit dispersed light are an appealing option. Thanks to their visual lightness, these accessories create a sensation of floating in space and become focal points.

La estancia es el espacio para lucir, por ello la importancia de planificar un buen diseño lumínico, en el que la luz decorativa es elemental. Entre los accesorios de iluminación más llamativos están las lámparas con pantallas translúcidas que emiten luz difusa. Por su escaso peso visual, estas piezas dan la sensación de estar flotando en el espacio, convirtiéndose en piezas focales.

Le séjour est une pièce qui doit faire de l'effet. Il est donc important de bien prévoir son éclairage avec une lumière décorative qui joue le premier rôle. Parmi les accessoires les plus séduisants, mentionnons les luminaires avec des parois translucides qui émettent une lumière diffuse. Parce que leur présence est discrète, on a l'impression qu'ils flottent dans l'espace pour attirer notre regard.

Das Wohnzimmer ist der Raum zum Vorzeigen, daher die Wichtigkeit eine gute Beleuchtung zu planen, in dem die dekorative Beleuchtung eine wesentliche Rolle spielt. Eine der schönsten Optionen sind Lampen mit lichtdurchlässigen Schirmen, die ein difuses Licht ausströmen. Durch ihr geringes optisches Gewicht, vermitteln diese Stücke den Eindruck im Raum zu schweben, sich damit in Blickfänge verwandelnd.

CHANDELIERS will transform a space thanks to the stylishness and sophistication they provide. The characteristic balls, the tear, bell, pineapple and almond shapes of their components and the strings of crafted glass beads (they can also be made from any other translucent material) hang from the arms to reflect the light with a spectacular zeal. If they are made of glass, it is a good idea for them to contain lead which enhances the luminosity.

LAS LÁMPARAS DE ARAÑA transforman el espacio, pues le aportan elegancia y sofisticación. Sus características bolas, lágrimas, campanillas, piñas, almendras o cadenetas de cuentas en cristal tallado (puede ser cualquier otro material translúcido) que penden de los brazos hacen que la luz se refleje con gracia. Cuando son de vidrio, hay que procurar que éste contenga plomo, pues el brillo es mayor.

LES LUSTRES transforment l'espace en lieu raffiné et sophistiqué. Qu'ils soient constituées à partir de petites sphères, de larmes, de clochettes, de pommes de pin, d'ovales ou de chaînettes en cristal taillé (ou en tout autre matériau translucide) suspendus à leur armature, la lumière peut s'y refléter avec grâce. Lorsqu'ils sont en verre, il faut s'assurer que ce dernier contient du plomb pour que leur éclat soit plus beau.

KRONLEUCHTER verändern den Raum, da sie Eleganz und Raffinesse beisteuern. Ihre charakteristischen Kugeln, Tränen, Glocken, Zapfen, Mandeln oder Ketten aus geschliffenem Kristall (es kann auch jedes andere durchsichtige Material sein), die von den Armen hängen, lassen das Licht mit Grazie reflektieren. Wenn sie aus Glas sind, sollte es Blei enthalten, da es dann stärker glänzt.

THE ESTHETIC QUALITIES of some lights turn them into sculptures in space that are truly a wonder to behold. Metal lights hanging from the ceiling in twisting and vibrant shapes suggest mobility. Others made of marble and onyx stand on the floor or on furniture and invigorate the patterns of the veining with back lighting.

POR SU ESTÉTICA, algunas lámparas son un real espectáculo para la vista y literalmente se convierten en esculturas espaciales. Las colgantes del techo, metálicas, de formas sinuosas y dinámicas, dan la impresión de movilidad. Otras hechas de mármol y ónix se apoyan en el piso o sobre algún muro para hacer lucir el dibujo del veteado mediante el recurso de iluminación posterior.

GRÂCE À LEURS QUALITÉS ESTHÉTIQUES, certaines lampes sont des réussites artistiques et se transforment en véritables sculptures. Les lampes suspendues au plafond, en métal, de formes ondulées et dynamiques, donnent du mouvement à la pièce. D'autres, en marbre et en onyx, reposent sur le sol ou sur un mur et leurs veines naturelles sont mises en valeur par un rétro-éclairage.

DURCH IHRE SCHÖNHEIT sind einige Lampen ein wirkliches Schauspiel für die Augen und werden zu Skulpturen im Raum. Hängelampen aus Metall mit gewagten und dynamischen Formen erwecken den Eindruck von Bewegung. Andere aus Marmor oder Onyx stehen auf dem Boden oder an einer Wand, um die Zeichnung der Maserung mit Beleuchung von hinten zu betonen.

THE LIGHT EMITTED BY FLOOR LAMPS is part of the decorative light scheme, as is the illumination provided by lights built in to the wall and spotlights used to provide radiance to announce the beauty of a work of art. Unlike the last two examples, whose beams can be directed as required, the direction of the light provided by floor lamps is determined by the shape of the screen.

LAS LUCES QUE EMITEN LAS LÁMPARAS DE PIE conforman parte de la luz decorativa, igual ocurre con las empotradas a muro y con aquellos puntos de luz orientados a exaltar la belleza de una obra de arte. A diferencia de estas dos últimas que irradian el haz de luz hacia donde se les dirige, en el caso de las lámparas de pie la dirección luminosa se da por la forma de la pantalla.

LES LUMIÈRES DIFFUSÉES PAR LES LAMPES à pied font partie de la décoration. C'est aussi le cas de celle émise par les lampes encastrées ou par quelques spots dirigés pour mettre en valeur un objet d'art. Mais contrairement à ces deux derniers types de luminaires à faisceau orienté, la direction de la lumière des lampes à pied dépend de la forme de l'abat-jour.

DAS LICHT VON STEHLAMPEN formt Teil der dekorativen Beleuchtung, genauso wie das Licht der in Wände eingelassenen Leuchten, oder auf Kunstwerke ausgerichtete, deren Schönheit herausstellende, Strahler. Im Gegensatz zu den beiden letzteren, deren Lichtstrahl ausgerichtet wird, wird bei Stehlampen die Beleuchtungsrichtung durch die Form des Schirmes bestimmt.

accent lighting
luz de acento
éclairage ponctuel
lichtakzente

THE JOB ENTRUSTED TO ACCENT LIGHTING is to highlight certain aspects of the decor, which means its presence in the living room is mandatory. It can be used in several ways. To bring out the texture and color of a wall, for instance, the best bet is lights shining upwards while a couple of downward-pointing lights make a sculpture on the floor really stand out.

LA TAREA DE LA LUZ DE ACENTO es resaltar algunos aspectos de la decoración, por lo que especialmente en la sala es indispensable. Se puede utilizar de varias formas. Por ejemplo, para exaltar la textura y el color de una pared lo ideal son algunas luminarias de luz ascendente, mientras que un par de luces descendentes hacen que destaque una escultura ubicada en el piso.

L'ÉCLAIRAGE PONCTUEL sert à faire ressortir certains détails de la décoration. Il est donc indispensable, en particulier dans un salon. Les formes des lampes ponctuelles sont variées. Pour mettre en valeur la texture et la couleur d'un mur, par exemple, les lampes à éclairage ascendant constituent ce qu'il y a de mieux alors que l'éclairage descendant de deux lampes fait bien ressortir une sculpture posée sur le sol.

MIT LICHTAKZENTEN UNTERSTREICHT man einen bestimmten Aspekt in der Dekoration, wodurch sie gerade im Wohnzimmer unerlässlich sind. Man kann sie auf verschiedene Weise verwenden. Zum Beispiel, um die Textur und die Farbe einer Wand hervorzuheben, sind einige Lampen mit hochscheinendem Licht ideal, während eine auf dem Boden stehende Skulptur durch ein paar herabscheinende Lampen hervorgehoben wird.

The light of a fireplace becomes the room's accent and makes its presence felt in the ambience every bit as much as table or wall lamps.

Cuando la chimenea está encendida, su luz se convierte en el acento de una habitación y cuenta tanto en el ambiente como la proveniente de lámparas de mesa y arbotantes.

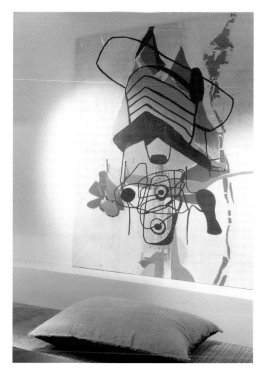

Lorsqu'une cheminée est allumée, sa lumière devient l'élément
le plus important de la pièce et participe autant à l'atmosphère
que les lampes de table ou d'applique.

Wenn der Kamin brennt, akzentuiert sein Licht den Raum und
ist genauso wichtig, wie das Licht der Tisch- oder Bogenlampen.

SOME SPECIALISTS IN LIGHTING prefer to use a number of equidistant points of light to accent different parts of the room and create a visual rhythm. A pair of illuminated and symmetrically located niches will reinforce this inflection and catch the eye of onlookers. They are also a great way to put the finishing touch to the living room's décor.

ALGUNOS DISEÑADORES DE ILUMINACIÓN prefieren colocar varios puntos equidistantes a través de los que se acentúen distintas áreas de la sala consiguiendo un ritmo visual. Un par de nichos iluminados y situados simétricamente refuerzan la cadencia y se convierten en elementos visuales que atraen la atención y son básicos para sellar la decoración de la sala.

CERTAINS DESIGNERS préfèrent placer plusieurs points lumineux à distance égale les uns des autres pour éclairer diverses zones du salon et, de cette manière, rythmer l'espace. Quelques cavités symétriques et illuminées renforcent ainsi la cadence visuelle, attirent l'œil et sont essentielles pour procéder à la décoration d'un salon.

EINIGE BELEUCHTUNGSDESIGNER bevorzugen es mehrere Lichtpunkte in gleichen Abständen anzubringen, durch die verschiedene Bereiche beleuchtet werden und ein optischer Rhythmus entsteht. Ein paar beleuchtete, symmetrisch angeordnete, Nischen verstärken den Rhythmus und werden zu attraktiven optischen Elementen, die wesentlich zum Abschluss der Dekoration eines Wohnzimmers beitragen.

THE STEPS on the staircase jut out and can be used as part of the lighting scheme with concealed lights placed under them that look good and are very practical. Care must be taken to choose the right potency and color for the lights, as these factors will determine the visual comfort and their impact on the décor.

LAS ESCALERAS que tienen peldaños con la huella volada se pueden aprovechar para que formen parte del diseño lumínico, pues éstos permiten instalar en la contrahuella luces ocultas que no sólo son muy estéticas, sino también funcionales. Es necesario cuidar la potencia y el color de la luminaria que se elija, pues de estos factores dependen el confort visual y el efecto en el decorado.

LES MARCHES éclairées d'un escalier peuvent être utilisées dans le cadre du design lumineux d'un salon. On dissimule alors des sources lumineuses dans les contremarches et l'effet est tout aussi esthétique que fonctionnel. Mais il est important de faire attention à l'intensité et à la couleur de la lumière car le confort visuel et leur apport dans le décor en dépendent.

TREPPEN, deren Stufen frei hängen, können als Teil des Beleuchtungsdesigns genutzt werden, da sie es erlauben unter den Stufen versteckte Lampen anzubringen, die nicht nur sehr ästhetisch sind, sondern auch funktionell. Bei der gewählten Lichtstärke und -wärme sollte man aufpassen, da von diesen Faktoren abhängt, wie angenehm sie fürs Auge sind und welchen Effekt sie auf die Dekoration haben.

A VERY LAIDBACK AMBIENCE can be achieved by using indirect lighting from several lights embedded into the ceiling. They should be low in potency or have a switch to regulate the power and the amount of light that may be required at any given moment. For optimum results, they should be distributed as symmetrically as possible around the living room.

ES FACTIBLE CONSEGUIR UN AMBIENTE muy relajado con luz indirecta a través de diversas lámparas empotradas a techo, cuya potencia sea baja o que tengan integrado un apagador que permita regular la energía e ir modulando la cantidad de luz según se desee a cada momento. Para que el resultado sea óptimo, las luminarias deben estar distribuidas lo más simétricas posibles en la sala.

SI L'ON VEUT QUE L'AMBIANCE de son salon soit très détendue, la lumière indirecte diffusée par plusieurs lampes encastrées au plafond est conseillée. L'intensité doit cependant rester faible. On peut aussi prévoir un variateur pour réguler la lumière à tout moment. Ajoutons que le résultat sera encore plus réussi si les sources lumineuses sont placées le plus symétriquement possible les unes des autres dans le salon.

MAN KANN EIN SEHR ENTSPANNTES AMBIENTE mit indirektem Licht durch mehrere in die Decke eingelassenen Lampen erreichen, deren Lichtstärke gering sein sollte oder die es erlauben die Lichtstärke nach den momentanen Wünschen zu verändern. Damit das Ergebnis optimal ist, sollten die Lampen so symmetrisch wie möglich über das Wohnzimmer verteilt werden.

indirect light
luz indirecta
éclairage indirect
indirektes licht

IF THE ENTRY OF DAYLIGHT is obstructed by translucent curtains, the light will be toned down and flow into the room more gently. This is a good way of making the living room comfortable by getting rid of bothersome glimmers but without undermining the room's clarity. The penetration of light will also be indirect if a door leading to other rooms with direct lighting is left open.

CUANDO LA ENTRADA DE LUZ NATURAL es interrumpida por una cortina translúcida, la luz se matiza y penetra con suavidad indirectamente al interior. Ésta es una buena solución para que la estancia se sienta confortable sin obstruir la claridad y con la que se eliminan molestos reflejos. La penetración también es indirecta si se deja abierta la puerta que dé hacia otras habitaciones que tengan luz directa.

LORSQU'UN RIDEAU TRANSLUCIDE interrompt l'entrée de la lumière naturelle, celle-ci est tamisée et pénètre indirectement et en douceur dans la pièce. Ce dispositif est recommandé pour faire de son salon une pièce confortable tout en conservant sa clarté et en éliminant les reflets gênants. La lumière pénètre également indirectement dans le séjour lorsqu'on laisse ouvertes les portes donnant sur des pièces éclairées directement.

WENN DER NATÜRLICHE LICHTEINFALL durch eine lichtdurchlässige Gardine gedämpft wird, wird das Licht matter und fällt weich und indirekt in den Innenraum. Das ist eine gute Möglichkeit, den Raum gemütlich wirken zu lassen ohne Helligkeit zu verlieren und man verhindert störende Reflektionen. Der Lichteinfall ist auch indirekt, wenn man Türen zu anderen Räumen mit direktem Lichteinfall offen lässt.

INDIRECT LIGHTING in which most of the light is aimed at the ceiling creates an effect similar to daylight. Pale colors on walls and bulky objects enhance this impression, which can be further increased by including highly polished surfaces that glint and glimmer.

LA ILUMINACIÓN INDIRECTA en la cual la mayor parte de la luz es dirigida hacia el techo, produce una luz que se parece mucho a la natural. Los colores claros en los muros y en objetos voluminosos ayudan a potenciar el efecto, y éste todavía se puede acrecentar más incluyendo superficies muy pulidas que eleven el grado de reflejo.

LORSQUE L'ÉCLAIRAGE INDIRECT est principalement dirigé vers le plafond, la lumière diffusée semble vraiment être naturelle. Les couleurs claires sur les murs ou sur des objets de grande taille accentuent encore ce phénomène, qui plus est avec des surfaces très lisses qui renforcent les reflets produits.

INDIREKTE BELEUCHTUNG, bei der der grösste Teil des Lichts auf die Decke gerichtet ist, lässt ein dem Natürlichen sehr ähnliches Licht entstehen. Helle Farben an den Wänden und bei grossen Objekten, helfen diesen Effekt zu verstärken und man kann ihn noch vergrössern, wenn man stark glänzende Oberflächen verwendet, die den Grad der Reflektion erhöhen.

daylight
luz natural
éclairage naturel
natürliches licht

IT IS WORTH MAKING an effort to draw daylight into a room as much as its orientation allows, to which end the windows should be large and allow plenty of light to pour in. At the same time, great care must be taken with the views and temperature, and furniture and wood need to be protected from possible damage caused by direct sunlight.

HAY QUE ESMERARSE por llevar la luminosidad natural dentro de la sala tanto como lo permita la orientación, tratando de que las ventanas sean de una dimensión generosa para que dejen entrar abundante luz. Sin embargo, es importante cuidar las vistas, proteger el interior de la incidencia térmica y evitar que por acción directa del sol se decoloren los muebles o se dañe la madera.

IL FAUT PRÉVOIR l'éclairage avec soin en étudiant bien l'orientation d'un salon pour profiter au maximum de la lumière naturelle à l'intérieur de la pièce. Il est nécessaire de prévoir, par exemple, une taille importante pour les fenêtres pour qu'elles laissent passer généreusement la lumière. Mais il est néanmoins indispensable de faire attention à la vue, de protéger le salon de la chaleur et d'éviter les rayons directs du soleil qui décolorent les meubles ou abîment le bois.

MAN SOLLTE BESTREBT SEIN, natürliches Licht, soweit es die Orientation zulässt, ins Wohnzimmer zu bringen, die Fenster so gross wie möglich sein zu lassen, um reichlich Licht hereinzulassen. Allerdings ist es wichtig sich vor Blicken zu schützen, den Innenbereich vor Wärmeverlust zu bewahren und zu vermeiden, dass direkter Sonneneinfall die Möbel bleicht oder das Holz schädigt.

A sprightly lighting scheme requires as much sunlight as possible during the day, and wall tones should be very pale to maximize luminosity

Si se busca un lugar vivificante, hay que procurar la mayor cantidad de luz natural durante el día, intentando que los muros sean de matices muy claros para que la luminosidad se intensifique.

Si l'on souhaite dynamiser son salon avec une lumière tonique, il est nécessaire que la plus grande quantité de lumière naturelle possible pénètre dans la pièce au cours de la journée avec des murs très clairs pour que la luminosité s'y réfléchisse.

Wenn man einen belebenden Bereich anstrebt, sollte man während des Tages so viel natürliches Licht wie möglich nutzen und die Wände so hell wie möglich sein zu lassen, um den Eindruck von Helligkeit zu verstärken.

DARK FURNITURE AND FLOORS absorb a lot of light, so it is a good idea to use them only if daylight is abundant. Floor to ceiling windows and L-shaped windows are ideal for letting light flood in from the outside. However if the light is direct then an architectural component that provides protection, such as a ceiling or a sunshade, should be included.

LAS MUEBLES Y LOS PISOS OSCUROS absorben mucha luz, por lo que es recomendable utilizarlos si la iluminación natural es cuantiosa. Los ventanales de piso a techo y aquellos en "L" son ideales para captar óptima luz del exterior; no obstante, cuando la luz pega directa es recomendable que se incluya algún elemento arquitectónico que brinde protección, ya sea un techo o un partesol.

LES MEUBLES ET LES SOLS FONCÉS absorbent énormément la lumière. On conseillera donc leur utilisation lorsque la lumière naturelle est abondante. Les grandes baies vitrées qui vont du sol au plafond et celles qui sont en forme de « L » sont idéales pour capter la plus grande quantité de lumière extérieure. Toutefois, lorsque le soleil éclaire directement la pièce, il est recommandé de la protéger avec quelques éléments architecturaux comme un toit ou un brise-soleil.

DUNKLE MÖBEL UND BÖDEN SCHLUCKEN viel Helligkeit, so dass sie nur zu empfehlen sind, wenn es reichlich natürliches Licht gibt. Fenster vom Boden bis zur Decke und solche in "L" Form sind ideal, um das Licht von Draussen zu nutzen; ohne Zweifel ist es bei direktem Sonneneinfall zu empfehlen irgendeinen baulichen Schutz einzuplanen, sei es ein Dach oder ein Sonnenverdeck.

Pure white is highly reflective, so much so that when sunlight hits it, a dramatic contrast between areas of light and shade is created.

El blanco puro posee índices de reflejo muy elevados, al punto que cuando la luz solar incide sobre él, el contraste lumínico de los juegos de luz y sombra se dramatiza.

La lumière se reflète tellement sur du blanc pur que lorsque le soleil l'éclaire, le jeu opposant ombre et lumière est encore plus net.

Reines Weiss hat eine sehr hohe Reflektionskraft, wodurch bei direktem Sonnenlicht, der Kontrast im Spiel zwischen Licht und Schatten dramatisch wirkt.

BLINDS HELP regulate the amount of daylight entering the room and afford privacy by just moving the slats. They are easy to use and to clean, and can be made from an extensive range of materials such as plastic, aluminum and wood. Most are very decorative and can create delightful interplays of light and shade.

LAS PERSIANAS SON COMPONENTES que ayudan a controlar la cantidad de luz natural y a dar privacidad con el simple hecho de entreabrir sus pestañas. Son sencillas de manipular y limpiar, y están hechas de materiales muy diversos como plásticos, aluminio y madera, y en su mayoría son altamente decorativas, pues al entrecerrar producen claroscuros inusitadas.

LES STORES SONT DES ÉLÉMENTS qui permettent de contrôler la quantité de lumière naturelle et d'obtenir un peu de clarté sans pour autant exposer la pièce à tous les regards. Faciles à manipuler et à entretenir, ils sont fabriqués avec des matériaux très variés comme les plastiques, l'aluminium et le bois. La plupart d'entre eux sont très décoratifs et, en les fermant à moitié, on obtient de somptueux clairs-obscurs.

JALOUSIEN HELFEN den naturlichen Lichteinfall zu kontrollieren und sichern, nur durch das halbe Schliessen ihrer Lamellen, die Privatsphäre. Sie sind einfach zu benutzen und sauberzumachen und es gibt sie in einer Vielzahl von Materialien, wie Plastik, Aluminium und Holz, und meistens sind sie sehr dekorativ, da, wenn halb geschlossen, ein ungewöhnliches Halbdunkel entsteht.

IF A WINDOW commands a stunning outdoor view, its virtues – in addition to illumination – will include turning the landscape into a decoration for the room, a kind of esthetic and luminous centerpiece. A well-oriented window should be free of curtains, the best option being rollable blinds if required.

CUANDO UNA VENTANA que da al exterior tiene una hermosa vista, el beneficio es único, pues además de ganar luz, el paisaje se convierte en una parte decorativa de la habitación; una especie de centro luminoso estético. Si la ventana está bien orientada, de preferencia se debe dejar sin cortinas que la cubran, en caso de que sea necesario, las persianas enrollables son la mejor alternativa.

QUAND LA VUE d'une fenêtre est très belle, il faut profiter de cet avantage parce que l'on gagne de la luminosité et que le paysage fait partie de la décoration du salon. Ce dernier devient alors une sorte de source lumineuse très esthétique. Lorsque la fenêtre est bien orientée, il est préférable de ne pas lui ajouter des rideaux et d'opter, si c'est nécessaire, pour des stores roulants.

WENN EIN FENSTER einen schönen Ausblick hat, ist das ein einzigartiger Vorteil, da, abgesehen von grösserer Helligkeit, die Landschaft zu einem Teil der Dekoration wird; eine Art ästhetische Lichtquelle. Wenn das Fenster gut ausgerichtet ist, sollte man es ohne verdeckende Gardine lassen, wenn es notwendig ist, sind aufrollbare Jalousien die beste Option.

dining rooms
comedores
salles à manger
esszimmer

WHEN IT COMES TO DINING ROOMS, indirect lighting is very much in vogue, but this is as much for its decorative contributions as for its practicality. A good option is lamps that reflect light towards the ceiling or lights concealed behind architectural components such as walls, false ceilings, niches, boxes or a perimeter molding.

LA ILUMINACIÓN INDIRECTA se ha puesto de moda en la decoración de comedores, pero más allá de su funcionalidad, se recurre a ella por intención decorativa. Esto se puede conseguir a través de lámparas que reflejen la luz hacia el techo o escondiendo fuentes de luz atrás de elementos de la arquitec-tura como muros y falsos plafones, nichos, cajillos o una moldura perimetral.

L'ÉCLAIRAGE INDIRECT pour la décoration des salles à manger est maintenant très à la mode et on y a principalement recours pour des raisons esthétiques. Dans ces cas-ci, on utilise par exemple des lampes avec une lumière dirigée vers le plafond ou des sources lumineuses dissimulées dans quelque élément architectural comme des murs, des faux-plafonds, des anfractuosités, des coffres ou des moulures autour de la pièce.

INDIREKTE BELEUCHTUNG ist in Esszimmern in Mode gekommen, aber jenseits ihrer Funktion, ist ihre Verwendung dekorativ. Man kann sie durch an die Decke strahlende, hinter baulichen Elementen, wie Mauern oder falschen Verkleidungen, Nischen oder Simsen, versteckte Lampen, erzielen.

indirect light
luz indirecta
éclairage indirect
indirektes licht

One good way to provide indirect lighting for the dining room is with a display case embedded in the wall with lights concealed at the back. In addition to illuminating the items it houses, a relaxing and romantic mood is achieved. At night, the lighting from the garden makes its way indoors creating an equally entrancing effect.

Una manera de iluminar indirectamente el comedor es a través de una vitrina que esté empotrada al muro con luminarias ocultas en su parte posterior. Aparte del lucimiento de los objetos que se encuentren en ella, se consigue la impresión de relajamiento y un toque romántico. Por la noche, la iluminación de los jardines recae indirectamente en el interior, también con un resultado mágico.

Des étagères vitrées encastrées dans le mur de la salle à manger et retro-éclairées par des lampes dissimulées sont un bon moyen pour disposer d'une lumière indirecte. Les objets présents sont mis en valeur et l'atmosphère de la pièce est à la fois détendue et romantique. Le soir, la lumière du jardin éclaire indirectement l'intérieur avec des effets magiques.

Eine der Möglichkeiten, den Esstisch indirekt zu beleuchten, ist durch eine in die Wand eingebaute Vitrine, mit versteckter Beleuchtung in ihrem oberen Teil. Von der Beleuchtung der DInge die sich in ihr befinden abgesehen, erreicht man eine entspannende Atmosphäre und einen Hauch Romantik. In der Nacht fällt die Beleuchtung des Gartens indirekt ins Innere, auch mit einem magischen Ergebnis.

THE MORE DELICATE the dining room's decorative lighting, the more stylish its setting will look. A good way to obtain such an elegant feel is with a couple of two-bulb wall lamps, whose beams gently illuminate the wall both upwards and downwards. For the best results, the tone of the light needs to be warmer than the wall. The effect can be taken further with candles.

CUANTO MÁS DELICADA es la luz decorativa del comedor, tanto más elegante se percibe su contexto. Para llegar a esta elegancia, una alternativa es incluir un par de arbotantes con doble foco, cuyo haz de luz bañe sutilmente el muro de forma ascendente y descendente. Es óptimo que la luz tenga un tono más cálido que el muro. La inclusión de velas realza el efecto.

PLUS L'ÉCLAIRAGE DÉCORATIF de la salle à manger est raffiné et plus l'élégance de cette pièce sera mise en valeur. Pour parvenir à un tel résultat, on peut opter pour deux lampes d'applique doubles dont l'éclairage ascendant et descendant habillera suavement le mur. Le ton de la lumière doit cependant être plus chaud que celui du mur. Et l'ajout de bougies renforce encore les effets produits.

JE DELIKATER die Beleuchtung des Esszimmers ist, um so eleganter wird die Umgebung empfunden. Um diese Eleganz zu erzielen, ist eine Möglichkeit einige Lampen mit doppelter Glühbirne zu verwenden, deren Lichtstrahl die Wand subtil in hoch- und herabscheinendes Licht badet. Optimal ist es, wenn das Licht einen wärmeren Ton hat, als der Farbton der Wand. Kerzen verstärken diesen Effekt.

decorative lighting
luz decorativa
éclairage décoratif
dekoratives licht

When it comes to heightening the sensation of spaciousness in a rectangular area, a safe bet is to use two symmetrical display boxes and shelves with decorative light on one of the shorter walls.

Una opción para aumentar la sensación de amplitud de un área de planta rectangular, es colocar dos vitrinas simétricas, con repisas con luz decorativa, en alguno de sus muros más cortos.

En installant deux meubles symétriques avec des étagères éclairées de manière décorative sur les murs les moins importants d'une salle à manger, on donne l'impression d'agrandir la pièce.

Eine Möglichkeit, um den Eindruck von Weite eines Bereiches mit rechteckigem Grundriss zu vergrössern, ist es zwei symmetrische Nischen, an deren Regalböden Leuchten angebracht sind, an einer seiner kürzeren Wände, einzubauen.

MIRRORS HAVE MUCH TO OFFER in a decorative lighting scheme, and can even become the star of the show. On the one hand, they can conjure up greater depth in space and, on the other, they step up the visual interplay of lights to create a sensation of warmth. A couple of stunning candelabras in front of a set of mirrors will provide some spectacular reflections.

LOS ESPEJOS SON IMPORTANTES en el diseño de la iluminación decorativa, incluso se pueden volver los elementos protagonistas del decorado. Por un lado, tienen la ventaja de evocar mayor profundidad espacial, por el otro, multiplican la relación visual de luminarias despertando calidez. Si se incluye un par de soberbios candiles frente a un grupo de espejos el escenario reflejado es inenarrable.

LES MIROIRS OCCUPENT UNE PLACE IMPORTANTE dans l'éclairage décoratif. Ils peuvent même y jouer le premier rôle. D'une part, ils approfondissent la pièce et, d'autre part, ils amplifient l'éclat des luminaires pour réchauffer l'espace. Et en plaçant deux lustres face à un ensemble de miroirs, l'effet produit est tel qu'il nous laisse cois.

SPIEGEL SIND IM DEKORATIVEM BELEUCHTUNGSDESIGN wichtig, sie können sich sogar in die Hauptdarsteller der Dekoration verwandeln. Auf der einen Seite haben sie den Vorteil eine grössere räumliche Tiefe zu vermitteln, auf der anderen Seite vervielfältigen sie die optische Beziehung zwischen den Lichtquellen, somit Wärme erweckend. Wenn man ein paar prächtige Kerzenhalter vor einer Gruppe Spiegel plaziert, ist die wiedergespiegelte Szene unbescheiblich.

daylight
luz natural
éclairage naturel
natürliches licht

Daylight is a wonderful guest in the dining room, especially at meal times, when the food will look at its most succulent. If light enters through a double height, it will bring out the full splendor of the texture of wood, a sizeable work of art or the surfaces of the table, floor and walls.

Para el comedor, la iluminación natural es un deleite, sobre todo al momento de disfrutar los alimentos, pues éstos lucen tal cual es en realidad su color. Si la luz accede por una doble altura, es la ocasión perfecta para exhibir las texturas de la madera, de alguna pieza de arte de gran formato, así como de las superficies de la mesa, pisos y paredes.

Pour une salle à manger, l'éclairage naturel est un bonheur, plus particulièrement au moment où l'on partage un repas car les teintes des aliments apparaissent alors telles qu'elles sont en réalité. Lorsque la lumière descend d'une pièce avec une double hauteur de plafond, il faut en profiter pour mettre en valeur la texture du bois, de certains objets d'art de grande taille et de quelques surfaces (table, sol, murs).

Im Esszimmer ist natürliches Licht eine Wonne, vor allem während man die Mahlzeiten geniesst, da diese ihre natürlichen Farben bewahren. Wenn das Licht durch ein Fenster doppelter Höhe eindringt, ist das eine perfekte Gelegenheit, um die Maserung des Holzes, eines grossflächigen Kunstwerkes, so wie die Oberflächen des Tisches, der Böden und der Wände, zur Schau zu stellen.

One way of increasing the sense of space in a rectangular area involves placing two symmetrical windows on any of its shorter walls, with shelves providing decorative light.

Una opción para aumentar la sensación de amplitud en un área de planta rectangular es colocar en alguno de sus muros más cortos dos vitrinas simétricas, con repisas que integren luz decorativa.

Une solution pour agrandir une pièce rectangulaire consiste à placer sur certains de ses murs les moins importants deux meubles symétriques avec des étagères éclairées décorativement.

Eine Möglichkeit, um den Eindruck von Weite eines Bereiches mit rechteckigem Grundriss zu vergrössern, besteht darin an einer seiner kürzeren Wände zwei symmetrische Nischen, an deren Regalböden Leuchten angebracht sind, einzubauen.

Closed doors comprising squares of glass and wooden frames separate two different settings but allow daylight to flow freely. When the doors are opened, the space is freed and the brightness increased.

Cuando están cerradas, las puertas con cuadrículas acristaladas y marcos de madera separan dos ambientes permitiendo el libre tránsito de la luz cenital; al abrirlas se libera el vano y se gana luminosidad.

Fermées, les portes avec des vitres en verre et une armature en bois permettent de séparer deux pièces à l'atmosphère différente sans interrompre le passage de la lumière. Ouvertes, l'espace s'agrandit et la luminosité augmente.

Wenn sie geschlossen sind, erlauben Türen mit quadratischen Fenstern und Holzrahmen zwei Bereichen voneinander zu trennen, ohne den Durchgang des Lichts zu stören; geöffnet gewinnt man Weite und Helligkeit.

DOUBLE CURTAINS limit the inflow of daylight into the dining room and increase its initimacy. Inner net curtains are usually made of materials with different levels of translucency. The outer curtains are made from thicker material and open up views, as well as framing and decorating the window. It's a good idea to hide the rails with an ornate object.

UNA ALTERNATIVA para restringir gradualmente el flujo de luz natural y obtener intimidad en el comedor es un doble cortinaje en la ventanas. Las cortinas interiores generalmente son de gasas con distintos niveles de translucidez. Las exteriores son de telas más gruesas y cuando están abiertas sirven de galería, además de enmarcar y decorar la ventana. Conviene ocultar sus rieles cubriéndolos con algún elemento de ornato

LES DOUBLES RIDEAUX aux fenêtres constituent un bon moyen de tamiser à sa convenance les rayons du soleil et de maintenir l'intimité de la salle à manger. Les rideaux intérieurs songénéralement en textiles plus ou moins transparents alors que ceux à l'extérieur sont fabriqués avec des tissus plus épais qui, ouverts, encadrent et décorent la fenêtre. Il est conseillé de dissimuler leur système d'ouverture et de fermeture par un élément décoratif.

EINE MÖGLICHKEIT allmählich den natürlichen Lichtfluss zu beschränken und Intimität im Esszimmer zu erreichen, ist durch doppelte Vorhänge an den Fenstern. Die Inneren sind normalerweise aus Gardinenstoff unterschiedlicher Lichtdurchlässigkeit. Die Äusseren sind aus gröberen Stoffen und wenn sie geöffnet sind, umrahmen und dekorieren sie die Fenster. Die Schienen sollton versteckt sein.

PALE TONES ON SURFACES ABSORB LESS LIGHT and assist daylight in its undertaking by reflecting brightness around the room. The opposite happens with darker colors. But even if the floor is dark, a generous helping of daylight and a white ceiling will infuse the atmosphere with luminosity.

AL ABSORBER MENOS LA LUZ, los tonos claros de las superficies se convierten en aliados de la luz natural, pues reflejan la luminosidad en el ambiente; lo contrario ocurre con los oscuros. Aun cuando el piso sea oscuro, una buena entrada de luz natural y un techo blanco hacen que se compense la luminiscencia de la atmósfera.

EN ABSORBANT MOINS LA LUMIÈRE, les teintes claires des surfaces deviennent les alliés de l'éclairage naturel car elles peuvent refléter la luminosité qui domine. Avec les couleurs foncées, l'inverse se produit. Même lorsque le sol est sombre, une source généreuse de lumière naturelle et un plafond blanc rétablissent la clarté de l'ensemble.

WENIGER LICHT ABSORBIEREND, sind helle Farbtöne auf den Oberflächen Verbündete des natürlichen Lichts, da sie die Helligkeit im Ambiente reflektieren; das Gegenteil passiert mit dunklen Farben. Auch wenn der Boden dunkel ist, gleichen reichlicher natürlicher Lichteinfall und eine weisse Decke die Beleuchtung im Ambiente aus.

accent lighting
luz de acento
éclairage ponctuel
lichtakzente

ART IS ALWAYS WELCOME and often plays a lead role in the décor. Its beauty can be brought out to the full with accent lighting. The number of lights used will depend on the size of the work of art. A large, brightly colored painting, for example, should be illuminated by a sufficient number of lights to bring any lurking shadows under control.

EL ARTE ES SIEMPRE BIENVENIDO y comúnmente adquiere un papel protagónico en la decoración. Se destaca aún más su belleza con unos acentos de luz. La cantidad de luminarias debe estar en función del tamaño de la obra, si es un cuadro de gran formato y posee un color encendido hay que incluir el número de lámparas suficiente para controlar las sombras.

LES OBJETS D'ART sont toujours les bienvenus et ils jouent, en général, le premier rôle dans la décoration d'une pièce. Leurs qualités esthétiques ressortent d'ailleurs mieux dans la lumière. Toutefois, le nombre de luminaires doit être en rapport avec la taille de l'objet : avec un tableau de grand format et de couleur vive, le nombre de lampes doit être suffisant pour contrôler les ombres présentes.

KUNST IST IMMER WILLKOMMEN und normalerweise steht ihr eine Hauptrolle in der Dekoration zu. Ihre Schönheit wird durch einige Lichtakzente noch hervorgehoben. Die Anzahl der Leuchten sollte im Verhältnis zur Grösse des Werkes stehen, wenn es sich um ein grossflächiges Bild handelt oder von einer leuchtender Farbe ist, sollte eine ausreichende Anzahl Lampen angebracht werden, um Schatten zu vermeiden.

bathrooms·baños
salles de bain·badezimmer

DAYLIGHT is essential in the bathroom, so it should be left as unobstructed as possible. A very practical way to ensure privacy and comfort, as well as to regulate the lighting, is by using wooden slats on the windows. If they are pure white, the sensation of brilliance will be all the more marked. Some cloth curtains in cold tones will create a contrast and add some vitality to the décor.

LA LUZ NATURAL es primordial para un baño, por lo que hay que intentar no interferir su paso. Una solución funcional para obtener privacidad y confort, así como para dosificar la iluminación son las puertas de persiana de madera. Si son de color blanco puro, la sensación luminosa aumenta. Para crear contraste y dar el toque a la decoración, se les puede colocar encima una cortinas textiles en tono frío.

LA LUMIÈRE NATURELLE est essentielle dans une salle de bain. Il faut donc essayer de ne pas l'entraver. Les portes-fenêtres avec des stores en bois sont, elles, un bon moyen de maintenir l'intimité de la pièce, d'en faire un espace confortable et de régler la luminosité. Blanc pur, elles n'en seront que plus éclatantes. Pour ajouter un petit plus à la décoration et créer un contraste, on peut les recouvrir avec des rideaux de couleur froide.

NATÜRLICHES LICHT ist im Badezimmer unabdingbar, deshalb sollte man seinen Zugang nicht behindern. Eine praktische Lösung sind Türen mit Holzlamellen, da sie Privatsphäre und Komfort sichern und das Licht dosieren lassen. Wenn sie aus weissem Holz sind, erhöht sich der Eindruck von Helligkeit. Um einen Konstrast entstehen zu lassen und der Dekoration einen besonderen Touch zu geben, kann man über ihnen einen Vorhang aus Stoff in einem kalten Farbton anbringen.

daylight
luz natural
éclairage naturel
natürliches licht

A HIGHLY DECORATIVE LOOK can be obtained in the bathroom with a few components such as rafters that block out some of the sun's rays and cast long shadows onto the walls. During the course of the day, the suns rays change, as do these shadows to produce an ambience of great vibrancy but also tranquility.

UN ASPECTO ALTAMENTE DECORATIVO en el baño se consigue interponiendo algunos elementos, del tipo de vigas, que cortan los rayos del sol provocando largas sombras que se dibujan sobre los muros. El sol pega a distintas horas del día de diferente forma, por lo que estas sombras también van cambiando haciendo sentir un ambiente vital, pero también de mucha paz.

EN INSÉRANT CERTAINS ÉLÉMENTS TRÈS DÉCORATIFS dans une salle de bain, par exemple des poutres apparentes qui arrêtent les rayons du soleil pour plonger dans l'ombre de larges pans sur un mur, les effets produits sont étonnants. Et comme le soleil n'éclaire pas la pièce de la même façon tout au long de la journée, les ombres obtenues se modifient également et apportent du dynamisme mais aussi une certaine paix dans l'espace.

EINEN HOCHDEKORATIVEN EFFEKT im Badezimmer erreicht man durch das Anbringen von Elementen wie Deckenbalken, die die Lichtstrahlen brechen und lange, auf die Wände gezeichnete Schatten verursachen. Je nach Tageszeit ändert sich die Form der Schatten, was das Ambiente lebendig, aber gleichzeitig friedlich wirken lässt.

THE COLOR WHITE complements the quality of daylight inside a room. If it is completely pure and used on most of the bathroom's surfaces, more than mere gleams, it will create a singular brilliance that evokes cleanliness and tidiness, thereby making it ideal for this space. Daylight increases the contrast between pure white and black to give the different depths a more solid definition.

EL COLOR BLANCO privilegia la calidad de la luz natural al interior del espacio, si es utilizado en su total pureza y en la mayor parte de las superficies del baño más allá de un reflejo, lo que se consigue un resplandor único que evoca orden y limpieza, y por ende, resulta muy adecuado para este sitio. La luz natural acentúa el contraste del blanco puro con el negro, lo que ayuda a definir profundidades.

LE BLANC très pur est un allié de la lumière naturelle lorsqu'il est utilisé à l'intérieur d'une salle de bain pour la plus grande partie de ses surfaces. Il ne réfléchit pas seulement la lumière, il illumine littéralement la pièce en lui donnant un aspect net et propre. C'est, de plus, une couleur qui convient bien à ce genre de lieu. Et la lumière naturelle accentue le contraste entre le blanc pur et le noir et approfondit l'espace.

DIE FARBE WEISS lässt natürliches Licht im Innenraum besonders zur Geltung kommen; wenn es in seinem reinsten Ton auf dem grössten Teil der Oberflächen des Badezimmers benutzt wird, spendet es, mehr als pure Reflektion, einen für diesen Bereich sehr angemessenen Glanz, der Ordnung und Sauberkeit vermittelt. Natürliches Licht betont den Kontrast zwischen reinem Weiss und Schwarz, was hilft die Tiefe zu definieren.

FLOOR TO CEILING WINDOWS and skylights provide uniform lighting that highlights the volumes and angles in the bathroom. If the design also features transparent structures, they will look like glass boxes that are brought to life when they come into contact with daylight and allow it to flow unhindered.

LAS VENTANAS ALTAS de piso a techo y los domos ofrecen una iluminación homogénea que hace que se destaque cada uno de los volúmenes y ángulos de un baño. Cuando en la solución de diseño se incluyen elementos transparentes, éstos se perciben como cajas de cristal que, además de vivificarse al contacto con la luz natural, permiten su libre tránsito.

LES BAIES VITRÉES qui vont du sol au plafond et les toits transparents permettent d'éclairer une salle de bain de manière homogène et font ressortir ses volumes et ses angles. Lorsque le design prévoit certains éléments transparents, ces derniers se transforment en coffres de verre qui s'animent au contact du soleil et qui laissent, en outre, passer la lumière.

HOHE FENSTER vom Boden bis zur Decke und Lichtdome bieten gleichmässige Beleuchtung, die alle Möbel und Winkel des Badezimmers herausstellt. Wenn man in die Dekoration transparente Elemente einschliesst, werden diese wie Glaskästen empfunden, die im Kontakt mit dem natürlichen Licht nicht nur lebendig erscheinen, sondern auch das Licht durchlassen.

indirect light
luz indirecta
éclairage indirect
indirektes licht

THE ATTRIBUTES OF INDIRECT LIGHT make it ideal for bathrooms by enriching its décor and accentuating its practical aspects. This light is not suitable for getting ready to go out, but it will afford the bathroom a touch of elegance. One way to make the most of it is by concealing lights behind a soffit or embedding an eye-catching display case with uniform light in the wall.

LA LUZ INDIRECTA tiene un comportamiento muy aplicable a los baños que enriquece su decorado y al mismo tiempo permite su funcionalidad. No es una luz que sirva para el arreglo personal, pero sí para brindarle al sitio una imagen elegante. Entre la opciones para conseguirla está ocultar las luminarias tras el plafón o empotrar a muro una vistosa vitrina cuya luz sea pareja.

L'ÉCLAIRAGE INDIRECT convient parfaitement aux salles de bains parce qu'il met en valeur la décoration présente tout en facilitant l'usage que l'on peut en faire. Cette lumière n'est certes pas idéale pour se regarder dans la glace mais elle dote la pièce d'une certaine élégance. Divers moyens existent pour disposer d'un tel éclairage : par exemple, dissimuler les luminaires dans le plafond ou encastrer, dans le mur, des étagères uniformément illuminées.

INDIREKTES LICHT lässt sich im Badezimmer gut anwenden, da es seine Dekoration bereichert und gleichzeitig funktionell ist. Dieses Licht kann man nicht zum Zurechtmachen benutzen, aber es gibt dem Raum ein elegantes Ambiente. Eine der Möglichkeiten ist es, Lampen hinter einer Platte anzubringen oder in der Wand eine Vitrine mit gleichförmiger Belouchtung einzubauen.

ALMOST WITHOUT EXCEPTION, lights that do not disclose their source will generate a charming effect. This can be very successfully accomplished by attaching a soffit to the ceiling with a perimeter molding in bas relief, and placing lights there to bathe the area in indirect light.

PRÁCTICAMENTE SIN EXCEPCIÓN, las fuentes de iluminación que no delatan su origen producen un encanto particular. Una solución con la que se alcanza un lindo efecto es construir en el techo un falso plafón con molduras perimetrales en bajo relieve, en donde se ubiquen algunas luces que alumbren indirectamente el área.

PRESQUE TOUTES LES LUMIÈRES dont il est difficile de localiser l'origine font de l'effet. Pour parvenir à une telle réussite, on peut installer un faux-plafond qui comportera des moulures tout autour et qui seront suffisamment en relief pour y dissimuler des lampes qui éclaireront indirectement la pièce.

PRAKTISCH OHNE AUSNAHME hat Beleuchtung, in der die Lampen nicht zu sehen sind, einen speziellen Charme. Eine Lösung, mit der man einen netten Effekt erzielt, ist es an der Decke eine falsche Verkleidung anzubringen, mit in sie eingelassenen Lampen, die den Bereich indirekt beleuchten.

HIGHLY POLISHED SURFACES, including transparencies and ornate objects made from reflective materials, create effects when they come into contact with light. These results need to be contemplated in the project because they are part of the indirect illumination. If the mirrors cover a whole wall, the sensation of spaciousness and depth will be all the greater.

LAS SUPERFICIES MUY PULIDAS, incluyendo transparencias y piezas de ornato de materiales reflejantes, emiten efectos al contacto con la luz; estos aspectos deben ser contemplados dentro del proyecto, pues forman parte de la iluminación indirecta. Si los espejos abarcan un muro, se gana percepción de amplitud y profundidad espacial.

LES SURFACES TRÈS LISSES, voire transparentes, et les objets décoratifs à base de matériaux réfléchissants s'animent au contact de la lumière. Lorsque l'on prévoit sa salle de bain, il faut prendre en compte ces effets car ils font partie de l'éclairage indirect. Quant aux miroirs sur les murs, ils donnent l'impression d'agrandir et d'approfondir la pièce.

STARK GLÄNZENDE OBERFLÄCHEN, einschliesslich durchsichtige und Dekorationsstücke aus reflektierendem Material, haben im Kontakt mit Licht einen Effekt; diese Aspekte müssen bei der Planung berücksichtigt werden, da sie Teil der indirekten Beleuchtung sind. Wenn die Spiegel über die gesamte Wand reichen, gewinnt man räumliche Weite und Tiefe.

IN A BATHROOM DECORATED in the contemporary style, a highly decorative outcome can be achieved with accent lighting if the functional components are emphasized by directing one of the lights onto the washbasin, with its beam skimming off the mirror, and another shining down onto a tray full of objects.

UNA BUENA OPCIÓN para obtener una iluminación de acento que derive en un logro decorativo dentro de un baño de estilo moderno es subrayar las partes funcionales dirigiendo una de las luminarias hacia el lavabo, intentando que el haz de luz pase rozando el espejo, y otra hacia el recipiente en donde estén puestas las amenidades.

SOULIGNER LE CÔTÉ FONCTIONNEL d'une salle de bain en éclairant, par exemple, un lavabo de style très moderne est un bon moyen pour utiliser l'éclairage ponctuel à des fins esthétiques. Dans ce cas-ci, le mieux est qu'un faisceau lumineux éclaire les contours du miroir alors qu'une seconde lumière mettra en valeur la vasque et ses accessoires.

EINE GUTE MÖGLICHKEIT Lichtakzente zu setzen, die einen dekorativen Wert im Badezimmer haben, ist es die Funktion der Elemente hervorzuheben, in dem man eine Lampe auf das Waschbecken richtet, dabei den Lichtstrahl über den Spiegel fallen lässt und eine andere auf den Bereich, in dem die Pflegeprodukte untergebracht sind.

accent lighting
luz de acento
éclairage ponctuel
lichtakzente

The color and texture of a wall can be emphasized by using two directable lights aimed at it. The cones of light this produces are a perfect way of providing a decorative touch.

Para enfatizar el color y la textura de un muro se incluyen dos luminarias dirigibles, orientando su potencia hacia la pared; el par de conos luminosos que se crean son perfectos para dar un toque decorativo.

Deux lampes dirigées vers le mur suffisent pour souligner l'esthétique de sa couleur et de sa texture. Les cônes de lumière ainsi obtenus sont parfaits pour apporter un plus dans la décoration de la pièce.

Um die Farbe und die Textur einer Wand hervorzuheben benutzt man zwei bewegliche Leuchten, die auf die Wand gerichtet sind; die beiden Lichtkegel, die dadurch geschaffen werden sind perfekt um der Dekoration einen besonderen Reiz zu verleihen.

Accent lighting can reinforce the different degrees of opacity of materials and define different planes of depth. In such cases, they can sometimes go at the front and other times at the back. Leds come in a good range of colors for creating a relaxing and intimate atmosphere in a minimalist setting.

A través de los acentos se puede sacar un beneficio de los diversos grados de opacidad de los materiales y definir los distintos planos de profundidad; para estos casos las luminarias se ubican unas veces al frente y otras en la parte trasera. Los led's tienen colores acertados para los ambientes minimalistas y con ellos se logra una atmósfera relajante e íntima.

Des lumières d'intensités variées peuvent mettre en valeur des matériaux plus ou moins opaques et les différentes profondeurs de la salle de bain. Pour parvenir à ce résultat, on place certains luminaires sur le devant de la pièce et d'autres dans le fond. Quant aux lampes à led, leurs couleurs conviennent tout à fait pour des atmosphères minimalistes, intimes et paisibles.

Durch Lichtakzente kann man die Dunkeltöne der Materialien nutzen und die verschiedenen Tiefen heraustellen; in diesem Fall platziert man die Leuchten entweder vor oder hinter den Objekten. LED Leuchten haben Farben, die zu minimalistischem Design passen und man erzielt mit ihnen eine entspannte, intime Atomosphäre.

LIGHTING can underscore the beauty of architectural components and emphasize the more eminent objects or materials. This is done through sources of light focusing on a specific surface or item of furniture. The key is not so much potency as beams that bestow a touch of distinction to the place.

CON ILUMINACIÓN es factible acentuar la belleza de los elementos arquitectónicos y conseguir que los objetos o materiales más importantes despunten. La manera de emplearla es a partir de fuentes de luz que se concentren en una determinada superficie o mobiliario. No se requiere potencia, sino haces de luz que le aporten al sitio un toque distintivo.

LA LUMIÈRE peut souligner la beauté des éléments architecturaux et mettre en valeur les objets ou matériaux les plus importants. Pour y parvenir, des sources de lumière dirigées vers des endroits ou des meubles spécifiques sont indispensables. Leur intensité ne doit pas forcément être élevée. Il faut simplement que les faisceaux lumineux produits apportent un plus dans la pièce.

MIT BELEUCHTUNG kann man die Schönheit der baulichen Elemente hervorheben und erreichen, dass die wichtigsten Objekte und Materialien betont werden. Das erreicht man durch die Konzentration des Lichts auf einer spezifischen Oberfläche oder einem Möbel. Man benötigt weniger Lichtstärke, als ein Licht, dass dem Bereich etwas Ungewöhnliches verleiht.

bedrooms
recámaras
chambres
schlafzimmer

indirect light
luz indirecta
éclairage indirect
indirektes licht

INDIRECT LIGHTING works wonders for the bedroom, thanks to its soft and relaxing charm. Wall and floor lamps can be placed to one side of the bed with their beams directed towards the ceiling. A set of translucent blinds will tone daylight and make it indirect.

EN LA HABITACIÓN viene muy bien la iluminación indirecta, pues con ella se consiguen luces suaves y relajantes. Los arbotantes y las lámparas de pie son funcionales a un lado de la cama y la direccionalidad de su luz es hacia el techo. La luz natural se convierte en indirecta al interponer una persiana translúcida que la matiza.

L'ÉCLAIRAGE INDIRECT convient bien aux chambres à coucher parce que la lumière obtenue est douce et apaisante. Les lampes d'applique ou à pied sont pratiques sur un des côtés du lit et elles éclairent l'endroit jusqu'au plafond. Quant à l'éclairage naturel, il peut être indirect si des stores translucides tamisent les rayons du soleil.

IM SCHLAFZIMMER ist indirekte Beleuchtung sehr angebracht, da man mit ihr weiches und entspannendes Licht gibt. Bogen- und Stehlampen sind an der Seite des Bettes funktionell und der Lichtstrahl sollte an die Decke gerichtet sein. Natürliches Licht wird zu indirektem, wenn man eine lichtdurchlässige Jalousie anbringt, die es dämpft.

FIREPLACES are decorative and, at the same time, a source of warmth. Their light is never still, thereby bringing a good measure of vitality into play in the bedroom. It also combines well with indirect light from other sources, such as an outdoor garden or light entering through a doorway.

LAS CHIMENEAS son un elemento decorativo y que al mismo tiempo brinda calidez. Su luminiscencia es movediza, con lo que también aporta la sensación de vitalidad en una habitación; se complementa bien con la luz indirecta proveniente de otras fuentes, pudiendo llegar a ser éstas, inclusive, las de algún jardín exterior o la que penetre por el vano de una puerta.

ÉLÉMENT DÉCORATIF par excellence, les cheminées réchauffent une chambre au propre comme au figuré. Et comme leurs flammes ne sont pas figées, elles dynamisent également la pièce. Traditionnellement associées à d'autres sources de lumière indirecte, celles-ci peuvent même provenir d'un jardin extérieur ou d'une porte ouverte.

KAMINE sind dekorative Elemente, die gleichzeitig Wärme geben. Ihr Licht ist in Bewegung, damit bringt man den Eindruck von Leben auch in den Raum; es lässt sich gut mit indirektem Licht aus anderen Quellen ergänzen, was sogar Licht sein kann, das von einem Garten oder durch eine offene Tür einfällt.

DEPENDING ON THE BEDROOM'S ORIENTATION, the season and the time of day, daylight makes its way into the bedroom through the windows directly or indirectly. If indirect white light is used indoors, a splendid distinction between indoors and outdoors will be created at sunset.

DEPENDIENDO DE LA ORIENTACIÓN LA RECÁMARA, de la estación del año y de la hora del día, la luz natural penetra directa o indirectamente por las ventanas. Si al interior se utilizan luminarias con luz blanca de una manera indirecta, la impresión que se genera entre el adentro y el afuera es muy agradable en los atardeceres.

TOUT DÉPEND DE L'ORIENTATION DE LA CHAMBRE, de l'heure de la journée et de la saison mais la lumière naturelle peut pénétrer directement ou indirectement par les fenêtres. Si la pièce est éclairée indirectement par des sources de lumière blanche, le contraste obtenu entre l'intérieur et l'extérieur est très agréable le soir.

VON DER AUSRICHTUNG DES SCHLAFZIMMERS, der Jahres- und Tageszeit, abhängig, fällt direktes oder indirektes Licht durch die Fenster ein. Wenn im Innenbereich Lampen mit weissem Licht in direkter Beleuchtung verwendet werden, ist der Eindruck der zwischen Drinnen und Draussen entsteht, in der Dämmerung sehr angenehm.

decorative lighting
luz decorativa
éclairage décoratif
dekoratives licht

Decorative techniques can harness daylight and transform it into an ornamental jewel. The variables in the room that need to be considered are the color and distribution of the furniture, the tone and finish of the surfaces, and, of course, the choice of decoration for the different openings. If everything is white, then the furniture will not obstruct the passage of light, and the results will be absolutely stunning with a large window.

A través de la decoración es posible manipular la luz natural y transformarla en decorativa. Las variables a controlar en el espacio son: el color y la distribución de los muebles, el tono y acabado de las superficies y, desde luego, la opción decorativa seleccionada para los vanos. Cuando todo es blanco, el mobiliario no interrumpe el tránsito lumínico y se tiene un enorme ventanal, el resultado es excepcional.

La lumière naturelle peut être modifiée pour devenir un élément de la décoration. Mais il faut bien contrôler les éléments suivants : la couleur et la distribution des meubles, la teinte et les finitions des surfaces et, bien évidemment, la décoration retenue pour les chambranles des portes et des fenêtres. Lorsque tout est blanc, le mobilier n'interrompt pas la circulation de la lumière et, avec une grande bais vitrée, le résultat est exceptionnel.

Durch die Dekoration kann man das natürliche Licht in ein dekoratives Element verwandeln. Die verschiedenen Möglichkeiten sind: die Farbe und die Anordnung der Möbel, Farbtöne und Material der Oberflächen, und natürlich die extremste Option. Wenn alles in Weiss gehalten ist, wird der Lichtfluss nicht von den Möbeln unterbrochen und wenn es ein riesiges Fenster gibt, ist das Ergebnis ausserordentlich.

OVER THE YEARS, bedside lamps have become a classic alternative for the bedroom thanks to the comfort afforded by being able to control them from the bed. If they are placed at the back of the bedside table, they will provide a decorative frame for the bed, as well as enhance the wall's appearance and coloring. Their height should be in proportion to the headboard.

A TRAVÉS DE LOS AÑOS, las lámparas de buró se convierten en una alternativa clásica para la habitación, ello se debe a la comodidad de ser operadas desde la cama. Si se colocan en la parte trasera de los burós enmarcan decorativamente la cama, además de resaltar el aspecto y colorido de la pared. Su altura debe estar en proporción con la de la cabecera.

AU FIL DES ANS, les lampes de chevet sont devenues de véritables éléments décoratifs dans les chambres. Il faut dire qu'elles sont bien pratiques une fois qu'on est couché. Placées dans la partie arrière des tables de nuit, elles encadrent merveilleusement le lit tout en mettant en valeur l'aspect et la couleur du mur. Mais leur taille doit être proportionnelle à celle de la tête de lit.

IM VERLAUF DER JAHRE haben sich Nachttischlampen, dank der bequemen Handhabung vom Bett aus, zu einer klassischen Beleuchtungsmöglichkeit im Schlafzimmer entwickelt. Wenn sie direkt an der Wand stehen, umrahmen sie, ausser das Aussehen und die Farbe der Wand zu betonen, sehr dekorativ das Bett. Ihre Höhe sollte in Proportion zum Kopfstück des Bettes stehen.

THERE IS NOTHING LIKE LIGHT and color to create an ambience with personality; at the end of the day, one gives rise to the other. There are many ways to use them in the décor. Red and earthen tones on the main surfaces and enlivened lighting make for a very warm atmosphere. The finishing touch is provided by a white light to create a contrast.

NADA MEJOR QUE CONSEGUIR UN AMBIENTE con personalidad a través de la luz y el color, a fin de cuentas, una origina al otro. Las aplicaciones en el decorado son muy amplias. Una atmósfera muy cálida se consigue con tonos rojos y térreos en las superficies dominantes y fuentes de iluminación candente. El toque final se logra con una luz blanca que actúe por contraste.

POUR PERSONNALISER UNE CHAMBRE, la lumière et la couleur représentent les meilleures options. D'ailleurs la première met en valeur la seconde. Ces deux éléments sont très utilisés en décoration. Par exemple, des tons rouges et terre, sur les surfaces principales, associés à des sources de lumière vive, réchauffent une chambre. Et on termine avec une lumière blanche pour apporter un peu de contraste.

NICHTS IST BESSER ALS EIN AMBIENTE mit Persönlichkeit durch die Beleuchtung und Farbe zu schaffen, letztendlich ist das Eine das Resultat des Anderen. Ihre Anwendung in der Dekoration ist sehr vielfältig. Eine sehr warme Atmosphäre erzielt man durch Rot- und Erdtöne in den Hauptflächen und eine kräftige Beleuchtung. Durch ein weisses Licht, das als Kontrast dient, erzielt man einen besonderen Reiz.

THE RIGHT COMBINATION of decoration, light and art will achieve unbeatable design results. Each sets aside its individual aspirations to join forces and raise the expression of the space to prominence. A sophisticated effect is achieved when a wall mimics a work of art hanging from the wall next to it. A clever use of light makes this possible.

UNA PRÁCTICA que conduce a insuperables resultados de diseño es entrelazar decoración, luz y arte. Cada aspecto traspasa su individualidad y participa en conjunto para que sea la expresión del espacio lo que descuelle. Esta idea puede ser muy sofisticada si un muro se mimetiza con una obra de arte colocada en la pared contigua, lo que en parte es posible gracias a la puntual intervención de la luz.

LORSQUE L'ON ASSOCIE DÉCORATION, lumière et objets d'art, le résultat obtenu est insurpassable. Chacun de ces éléments agit individuellement et mais aussi l'un par rapport aux autres pour faire de la pièce un endroit exceptionnel. Il est ainsi très élégant de placer un tableau qui se fond dans un mur grâce à la lumière ponctuelle.

EINE PRAKTIK, die zu unübertroffenen Ergebnissen im Design führt, ist es Dekoration, Licht und Kunst miteinander zu verbinden. Jedes steuert seine Individualität bei und zusammen lassen sie den Charakter des Raumes entstehen. Es ist sehr raffiniert, wenn eine Wand ein Kunstwerk an der benachbarten Wand kopiert. Das ist dank der sehr präzisen Beleuchtung möglich.

The effect of the light makes a bedroom feel cozy. The glints, the floor lamps with white light and a well-lit painting are part of the décor.

Los efectos luminosos van haciendo que una recámara se sienta acogedora. Los destellos, las lámparas de pie con luz blanca y un cuadro bien iluminado conforman parte del decorado.

Les effets de la lumière participent à l'aspect douillet d'une chambre. L'éclat des luminaires, les lampes à pied avec une lumière blanche et un tableau bien éclairé font ainsi partie du décor.

Die Beleuchtung macht es möglich, dass ein Schlafzimmer gemütlich wirkt. Die Lichtreflektionen, die Stehlampen mit weissem Licht und das Gemälde sind Teil der Dekoration.

daylight
luz natural
éclairage naturel
natürliches licht

NOWHERE IS DAYLIGHT RECEIVED with such gratitude as in the bedroom, but it is precisely because of this that it needs to be regulated. This can be done with a number of decorative objects including blinds, curtains, double curtains, walls, furniture, building materials, along with many others. Colors are reflected naturally in the absence of filters.

SI EN ALGÚN LADO ES BIENVENIDA LA LUZ natural es en la habitación, pero precisamente por eso debe de tener la posibilidad de ser modulada. Con distintos elementos decorativos y arquitectónicos es factible modificarla; persianas, cortinas, doble cortinaje, muros, mobiliario y materiales de construcción son solamente algunos de ellos. Los colores se reflejan mas naturalmente en donde no existen filtros.

S'IL EXISTE UNE PIÈCE POUR LA LUMIÈRE NATURELLE, c'est bien la chambre. Mais cette lumière doit pouvoir être modulée. Grâce à certains éléments décoratifs et architecturaux comme, par exemple, les stores, les rideaux, les doubles-rideaux, les murs, les meubles et les matériaux de construction, il est possible de le faire. Et les couleurs se reflètent naturellement dans les endroits qui ne sont pas tamisés.

WENN ES EINEN RAUM GIBT, in dem natürliches Licht willkommen ist, ist es das Schlafzimmer, aber genau deshalb sollte man die Möglichkeit haben es zu kontrollieren. Mit verschiedenen Elementen der Dekoration und der Architektur es das möglich: Jalousien, Gardinen und Vorhänge, Wände, Möbel und Materialien sind nur einige. Die Farben wirken natürlich, wenn das Licht nicht gefiltert wird.

The importance of orienting the bed towards where the light enters depends on the visuals. If there are no good views available or if the luminosity needs to be toned down, then the window should be covered. If the window is floor to ceiling, a good option is to use translucent, rollable net curtains, but curtains made with cloth as opaque as the task requires can also do the job perfectly well.

La importancia de que la cama mire hacia donde está la entrada de luz está en las visuales; si no se tienen vistas o se quiere graduar la luminosidad lo mejor es vestir la ventana. Entre las alternativas para cubrir una ventana de piso a techo están las cortinas enrollables de malla translúcida, pero también se puede usar cortinaje de telas tan opacas como se prefiera.

Il est important que le lit soit dirigé vers les sources de la lumière naturelle. Lorsque la vue n'est pas agréable ou si l'on souhaite tamiser la luminosité, il vaut mieux habiller les fenêtres. On peut alors opter pour des rideaux à tissus voilés ou à toiles plus opaques qui vont du sol au plafond.

Das Wichtige an der Ausrichtung des Bettes zum Fenster ist die Aussicht; wenn es keine gute Aussicht gibt oder man die Helligkeit dämpfen möchte, ist es am besten das Fenster zu bedecken. Eine der Möglichkeiten ein von Boden bis zur Decke reichendes Fenster zu bedecken, ist durch ein Rollo mit einem lichtdurchlässigem Netz, oder man kann auch Vorhänge in der gewünschten Dunkelheit verwenden.

SUNLIGHT ENTERING a bedroom is uniform. This makes the décor look very natural. Polished whitish floors lend their weight to this effect, as do pure white bed linen and furniture. Color, including black, can go on walls at right angles to the point of daylight.

LA LUZ SOLAR que accede indirectamente a una habitación es pareja. Este efecto hace que el decorado se perciba muy natural. Los pisos pulidos y blanquecinos cooperan a que no se pierda el objetivo, así como la ropa de cama y el mobiliario en blanco puro. El color, incluso el negro, puede ir en los muros que hacen ángulo recto con el vano.

LORSQUE les rayons du soleil pénètrent indirectement dans une chambre, la lumière y est uniforme et la décoration choisie paraît être très naturelle. Les sols crème et lisses participent à cet effet, tout comme une literie et des meubles blanc pur. D'autres couleurs, comme le noir, peuvent être appliquées sur des murs à angle droit par rapport aux chambranles des portes et fenêtres.

INDIREKTES Sonnenlicht, das in den Raum einfällt, ist gleichmässig. Dieser Effekt lässt die Dekoration sehr natürlich erscheinen. Glänzende, weisse Böden steuern dazu bei, dieses Ziel zu erreichen, so wie auch die Bettwäsche und die Möbel in reinem Weiss. Farben, einschliesslich Schwarz kann auf Wänden verwendet werden, die einen rechten Winkel mit dem Fenster bilden.

A frame in the form of an attractive molding can turn a window into a picture. Light from the outside catches the eye and directs it towards nature's very own works of art.

Una ventana se torna en un cuadro si se le coloca una moldura protagónica como marco. La luminiscencia exterior atrapa la vista y la conduce hacia una obra artística de la naturaleza.

Une fenêtre peut prendre l'apparence d'un tableau si son encadrement est décoratif. La lumière extérieure capte alors les regards pour nous faire comprendre que la nature est une véritable œuvre d'art.

Ein Fenster kann wie ein Gemälde wirken, wenn man es mit einem Sims umrahmt. Die Helligkeit draussen fängt den Blick ein und lenkt ihn auf das Kunstwerk Natur.

Blinds consisting of thin, horizontal and movable slats are highly decorative. They also have the added benefit of being able to block the entry of daylight either in part or in full, as well as directing it towards the front, the floor or the ceiling. In addition, they produce enchanting shadows. Another way to regulate sunlight is by using curtains.

Las persianas horizontales de tablillas móviles y delgadas son altamente decorativas, poseen la ventaja de que pueden bloquear total o parcialmente el paso de la luz natural y dirigirla hacia el frente, el piso o el techo. Tienen además la cualidad de generar sombras encantadoras. Otra alternativa para el control de la luz solar son unas cortinas.

Les stores à fines bandes horizontales sont très décoratifs et présentent l'avantage de pouvoir bloquer partiellement ou totalement la lumière naturelle et la diriger ailleurs, vers le plafond ou le sol. Ils donnent, en outre, naissance à des ombres époustouflantes. Les rideaux constituent également un moyen de contrôler les rayons solaires.

Horizontale Jalousien mit beweglichen schlanken Lamellen sind hochdekorativ und haben den Vorteil, dass sie das Einfallen natürlichen Lichts vollständig oder teilweise blockieren können oder es gerade, zum Boden oder zur Decke leiten können. Ausserdem schaffen sie bezaubernde Schatten. Eine andere Möglichkeit das Eindringen von Sonnenlicht zu steuern sind Vorhänge.

CURTAINS play an essential role in getting the atmosphere just right. They can do this in a number of ways. One is to get them to blend into the architecture, by making them made to measure and fixing them to the window frames. If they are transparent they will make reading or working easier by toning down the light and preventing glints.

LAS CORTINAS se constituyen en elementos trascendentes para conseguir la atmósfera anhelada. Hay varios caminos al seleccionarlas. Uno de ellos es provocar su integración a la arquitectura, haciéndolas a medida del espacio y empotrándolas a los marcos de las ventanas. Si son transparentes facilitan las tarea en los espacios de trabajo o lectura, pues suavizan la luz y evitan reflejos.

LES RIDEAUX sont on ne peut plus importants pour obtenir l'atmosphère désirée. On peut retenir différents critères pour les choisir. On peut décider de les insérer dans le décor en les préférant de même proportion que la chambre et encadrés par les fenêtres. S'ils sont transparents, ils conviennent mieux aux espaces pour travailler et pour lire parce que la lumière sera adoucie et les reflets inexistants.

VORHÄNGE sind ein wichtiges Element, um die gewünschte Atmosphäre zu erhalten. Es gibt mehrere Möglichkeiten sie auszuwählen. Eine davon ist es, sie in die Architektur zu integrieren, sie nach Mass anfertigen zu lassen und sie in den Rahmen der Fenster einzubauen. Durchsichtige Gardinen sind besser für Arbeits- oder Lesebereiche, da sie das Licht etwas dämpfen und Reflektionen verhindern.

terraces
terrazas
terrasses
terrassen

TERRACES are outdoor areas in which light plays a major role in the décor. At night a singular effect can be created by placing upward-pointing lights in a pool or in front of sculptures or other shapely objects. Their veining, shape, texture and color will also be highlighted on stone surfaces.

LAS TERRAZAS son exteriores particularmente susceptibles de decorar con iluminación. Por la noche la impresión es única si se ubican luces ascendentes, ya sea dentro de un espejo de agua o frente a algunos objetos escultóricos. Si los recubrimientos son de piedra, su veteado, forma, textura y color también se enfatizan.

LES TERRASSES sont des espaces extérieurs très faciles à décorer par l'intermédiaire de la lumière. De nuit, les effets créés sont uniques si on place des sources de lumière ascendante, soit dans un miroir d'eau, soit face à quelque sculpture. Si le revêtement de la terrasse est en pierre, l'éclairage fera également ressortir les veines naturelles, la forme, la texture et la couleur.

TERRASSEN sind Aussenbereiche, die sich besonders für die Dekoration mit Beleuchtung anbieten. Nachts erreicht man einen einmaligen Eindruck, wenn man aufsteigende Leuchten, entweder an einem Wasserspiegel oder gegenüber einer Skulptur anbringt. Wenn die Mauern aus Stein sind, kommt ihre Maserung, Form, Textur und Farbe auch besonders zur Geltung.

decorative lighting
luz decorativa
éclairage décoratif
dekoratives licht

Visually appealing results can be achieved if light comes into contact with a swimming pool, pond or the surface of some other body of water that mirrors the landscape.

Un recurso que resulta muy atractivo a la vista es cuando al contacto con la luz una alberca, espejo de agua o cualquier otra superficie acuosa duplica el paisaje.

Les piscines, miroirs d'eau et autres bassins sont des accessoires décoratifs très esthétiques car, grâce à la lumière, ils peuvent réfléchir le paysage environnant.

Ein sehr attraktives Mittel ist es, wenn ein Schwimmbecken, ein Wasserspiegel oder jegliche andere Wasserfläche, bei dem Kontakt mit Licht die Landschaft wiederspiegelt.

indirect light
luz indirecta
éclairage indirect
indirektes licht

INDIRECT DAYLIGHT or artificial light offers ways of defining an overall ambience for the terrace. The lighting of surrounding plants, trees and bushes is particularly significant in these outdoor designs because of their visual relevance in the terrace and the rich warmth they generate.

LAS ENTRADAS INDIRECTAS DE LUZ, tanto natural como eléctrica, se usan para conseguir un ambiente general en la terraza. En estos diseños exteriores adquiere una especial relevancia la iluminación de las plantas, árboles y arbustos circundantes, pues su resplandor tiene un peso visual en la terraza y la dota de una rica sensación de calidez.

ON UTILISE LES SOURCES DE LUMIÈRE INDIRECTE (naturelle ou électrique) pour doter la terrasse d'une ambiance particulière. Dans le cadre de ces décorations extérieures, l'éclairage des plantes, des arbres et des arbustes dans la périphérie est très efficace car leur éclat attire l'œil sur une terrasse et réchauffe agréablement cet espace.

INDIREKTER LICHTEINFALL, sowohl natürlicher als auch künstlicher, benutzt man, um ein generelles Ambiente auf der Terrasse zu schaffen. In diesem Design eines Aussenbereiches kommt der Beleuchtung der Pflanzen, Bäumen und umgebenden Büschen eine besondere Rolle zu, da sein Lichtschein optisches Gewicht für die Terrasse hat und ihr einen wohltuend warmen Eindruck verleiht.

A terrace can be provided with indirect lighting when most of the light comes from inside the house or when low-intensity floor lights are used.

La iluminación indirecta de una terraza puede generarse cuando hay un dominio de la luz que emana del interior, o bien, a través de luminarias a piso, cuya intensidad lumínica sea baja.

On peut éclairer indirectement une terrasse grâce à une importante lumière qui provient d'une pièce intérieure ou par le biais de luminaires de faible intensité au sol.

Man kann indirekte Beleuchtung auf der Terrasse durch die Kontrolle des Lichtes, das von Innen auf sie fällt, oder auch durch Leuchten im Boden mit schwacher Lichtstärke, errreichen.

IF INDOOR LIGHTING that is soft and warm and yellowish in color reaches the terrace outside, it will provide it with a cozy atmosphere. The lighting scheme is crowned with a fireplace emitting strong, variable illumination, together with a few accents of light scattered around the area.

CUANDO EL COLOR DE LA ILUMINACIÓN interior es cálido e irradia luz suave y amarillenta, ésta transita al espacio exterior brindándole a la terraza una atmósfera confortable. El diseño de iluminación se completa con una chimenea que emite luz fuerte e inestable, y algunos acentos de luz esparcidos en el área.

LORSQUE L'ÉCLAIRAGE intérieur est chaud et diffuse une lumière douce aux reflets cuivrés, l'espace extérieur est lui aussi illuminé et le confort de la terrasse n'en est que plus apparent. On peut alors compléter le design de l'éclairage par la lumière forte et mouvante d'une cheminée et par quelques points lumineux disséminés ici et là.

WENN DIE BELEUCHTUNG im Innenbereich warm ist und ein saftes, gelbliches Licht abstrahlt und dieses nach Aussen fällt, gibt es der Terrasse eine angenehme Atmosphäre. Das Design wird durch einen Kamin vervollständigt, der starkes, unstetiges Licht abgibt und einige Lichtakzente über den Bereich verteilt.

daylight
luz natural
éclairage naturel
natürliches licht

DAYLIGHT blesses outdoor areas with a magical touch, by highlighting their architectural volumes through an interplay of light and shade. One of its main decorative attributes is the shadows it hurls onto walls and floors, which change in size as the day wears on.

LA LUZ NATURAL le imprime un toque de magia a los espacios exteriores, porque permite el lucimiento potencial de los volúmenes de la arquitectura a través del juego de claroscuros. Uno de sus atractivos con mayor repercusión desde la óptica de lo decorativo son las sombras que se generan sobre muros y pisos, cuyo tamaño varía según la hora del día.

LA LUMIÈRE NATURELLE apporte une certaine magie aux espaces extérieurs parce qu'elle se traduit par un éclairage intense des volumes de l'architecture grâce au jeu des clairs-obscurs. Un de ses avantages esthétiques les plus importants pour les yeux réside dans le fait qu'elle génère des ombres sur les murs et au sol dont la taille varie en fonction de l'heure.

NATÜRLICHES LICHT gibt den Aussenbereichen einen Hauch Magie, da es erlaubt das Potential der baulichen Struktur vollständig, durch das Spiel mit Hell und Dunkel, zu nutzen. Eine der, aus der Sicht der Dekoration gesehen, grössten Wirkungen haben die Schatten auf Wänden und Böden, deren Grösse je nach Tageszeit variiert.

IF THE TERRACE IS DESIGNED as a place for socializing in and not for contemplation, the shade afforded by gazebos, sunshades, marquees and verandas will be essential to lessen the sun's intensity. Rafters are practical because they can be covered by different materials or plants, and the shadows they produce are part of the lighting scheme.

SI LA TERRAZA ESTÁ PLANEADA como un espacio donde estar y no como una zona para contemplar, es imprescindible incluir sombras del tipo de pérgolas, sombrillas, carpas y verandas, que ayuden a mitigar la intensidad del sol. Las vigas son funcionales porque se pueden cubrir con distintos materiales o bien con plantas, y el sombreado que provocan también es parte del diseño lumínico.

SI L'ON CONSIDÈRE QUE LA TERRASSE est un lieu pour passer des bons moments et pas simplement pour contempler la vue, il est indispensable d'y aménager des zones à l'ombre avec une pergola, des parasols, des bâches ou une véranda afin d'atténuer la chaleur du soleil. Éléments d'abord fonctionnels, les poutres peuvent être recouvertes par divers matériaux ou par des plantes qui participent aussi au design de l'éclairage.

WENN DIE TERRASSE als ein Bereich geplant ist, in dem man sich längere Zeit aufhält, ist es unerlässlich Schatten durch Pergolas, Sonnenschirme und Zeltdächer, einzuplanen, die helfen die Intensität der Sonneneinstrahlung zu mildern. Balken sind sehr praktisch, da sie mit verschiedensten Materialien, oder sogar mit Pflanzen, bedeckt werden können und ihr Schatten Teil des Designs ist.

exteriors
exteriores
extérieurs
aussenbereiche

accent lighting
luz de acento
éclairage ponctuel
lichtakzente

ACCENT LIGHTING is very useful for emphasizing one aspect or another on the outside of the building. If it is sizeable, its height can be highlighted with powerful lights shining upwards. Warm-colored light is excellent for the job, especially when used to illuminate a stone surface.

LA LUZ DE ACENTO se aprovecha para que alguno u otro aspecto de la fachada descuelle. Para recalcar la altura de algún volumen de la edificación se usan luminarias de alta potencia con dirección ascendente. Especialmente las luces cálidas vienen muy bien en estas circunstancias, sobre todo si el cuerpo iluminado es de materiales pétreos.

L'ÉCLAIRAGE PONCTUEL est très utile pour mettre en valeur tel ou tel aspect de la façade. Lorsque la bâtisse est très élevée, on optera pour des luminaires de forte intensité à lumière ascendante afin d'en souligner la hauteur. On peut ajouter quelques sources de lumière chaude, surtout si la demeure éclairée est en pierre.

LICHTAKZENTE können sehr gut genutzt werden, um den einen oder anderen Aspekt der Fassade herauszustellen. Wenn das Gebäude sehr hoch ist, kann man dies durch sehr starke Leuchten mit hochscheinendem Licht betonen. Besonders geeignet sind dafür Lampen mit warmen Licht, insbesondere wenn die Fassade aus Stein ist.

If the ceiling, rafters or any horizontal component of a terrace is visually significant, this can be offset by illuminating the top.

Si el techo, la viguería o cualquier elemento horizontal de una terraza tiene un peso visual importante, esta característica se compensa reforzando la altura con luz.

Lorsque le toit, les poutres ou tout autre élément horizontal attire trop les regards sur une terrasse, il est possible de compenser cet excès en plaçant les sources de lumière à une grande hauteur.

Wenn das Dach, die Balken oder irgendein anderes horizontales Element einer Terrasse ein bedeutendes optisches Gewicht hat, kann man es durch die Betonung der Höhe mit der Beleuchtung ausgleichen.

If light sources are concealed among plants, the lighting will be more subtle and not overwhelm the setting. The building will also look lighter if its facade features transparent components transmitting light outdoors. These two decorative options, when combined, will achieve splendid results.

Cuando se ocultan las fuentes luminosas entre las plantas la iluminación apenas se sugiere y no contamina el lugar. Si la fachada de la vivienda tiene elementos transparentes que emiten luz al exterior, la construcción se percibe más ligera. Con la fusión de estas dos opciones decorativas se llega a un resultado espléndido.

En dissimulant les sources de lumière dans des plantes, l'éclairage est comme suggéré et ne compromet pas la beauté des lieux. Et lorsque la façade de la demeure est dotée d'éléments transparents laissant passer de la lumière vers l'extérieur, la maison a l'air plus léger. Si l'on sait associer ces deux solutions décoratives, le résultat ne peut être que splendide.

Wenn Lichtquellen zwischen Pflanzen versteckt werden, wird Beleuchtung nur angedeutet und drängt sich nicht auf. Hat die Fassade lichtdurchlässige Elemente, die Licht nach Aussen dringen lassen, wird ein Gebäude als leichter empfunden. Mit der Kombination dieser beiden Dekorationsmittel erzielt man einen hervorragenden Effekt.

IF THE SOURCES OF LIGHT are concealed among plants, the light will be more suggestive than an actual source of illumination, and it will not drown the place in luminosity. If the outside of the house features transparent components through which light emerges, the building will look lighter. Spectacular results are provided when these two options are used together.

CUANDO SE OCULTAN LAS FUENTES LUMINOSAS entre las plantas producen una iluminación que se sugiere, sin contaminar el lugar. Si la fachada de la vivienda tiene elementos transparentes que emiten luz al exterior, la construcción se percibe más ligera. La fusión de estas dos opciones decorativas se llega a un resultado espléndido.

DISSIMULÉES ENTRE DES PLANTES, les sources de lumière éclairent discrètement un endroit sans en altérer l'aspect. Lorsque la façade d'une construction est dotée d'éléments transparents qui diffusent de la lumière vers l'extérieur, la bâtisse semble plus légère. Et en combinant ces deux techniques décoratives, le résultat est splendide.

WENN DIE LEUCHTEN zwischen den Pflanzen angebracht werden, spenden sie ein angedeutetes Licht, ohne den Bereich zu überlagern. Wenn die Fassade des Hauses durchsichtige Elemente aufweist, die Licht nach Aussen fallen lässt, wirkt das Gebäude leichter. Die Verbindung dieser beiden dekorativen Mittel führt zu einem grossartigem Ergebnis.

indirect light
luz indirecta
éclairage indirect
indirektes licht

ONE HIGHLY DECORATIVE possibility involves making the most of the lighting coming from indoors onto a façade made of glass from floor to ceiling. The light is indirect so it will envelope and frame the outdoor landscape. If its design is virtually horizontal and comprises stones, aquatic plants and sand, the monoliths of light will become a focal point in this serene setting.

UNA TÉCNICA DECORATIVA consiste en sacar ventaja del alumbrado procedente del interior de una fachada acristalada de piso a techo. Al ser indirecta, la iluminación envuelve y enmarca el paisaje exterior. Si éste posee un diseño casi horizontal, limitado a piedras, plantas acuáticas y arena, los monolitos de luz se vuelven una especie de centros vitales para este ambiente sereno.

PROFITER DE L'ÉCLAIRAGE intérieur d'une façade en verre du sol au toit est une technique décorative qui a fait ses preuves. Indirecte, la lumière entoure et délimite le paysage extérieur. Lorsque ce dernier est de forme presque horizontale avec des pierres, des plantes aquatiques et du sable, les blocs de lumière se transforment en sources de vie dont la lumière irrigue sereinement tout l'espace.

EINE TECHNIK in der Dekoration besteht darin, die Vorteile der Beleuchtung von Innen, einer Glasfassade die sich vom Boden bis zum Dach erstreckt, zu nutzen. Wenn diese ein fast horizontales Design aufweist, durch Steine, Wasserpflanzen und Sand, begrenzt wird, werden die Monolithen aus Licht zum lebendigen Zentrum in dieser gelassenen Atmosphäre.

ALL ARCHITECTURAL COMPONENTS produce an effect when they come into contact with light. Solid surfaces obstruct its passage, while openings release it. Some can scatter it in highly attractive ways, for instance wicker blinds that reveal light filtering out through the gaps, or any opening of any size in the building.

TODOS LOS COMPONENTES de la arquitectura tienen un efecto ante la luz. Los macizos impiden su paso y los vanos la dejan libre. Algunos se pueden convertir indirectamente en sus difusores más atractivos, comenzando por las rejillas que dejan ver la luz que se cuela por sus agujeros, hasta cualquier apertura de la construcción, sin importar su tamaño.

CHAQUE ÉLÉMENT architectural réagit de façon particulière au contact de la lumière. Massifs, ils l'empêchent de passer mais, ouverts, ils lui laissent le passage. Certains peuvent se transformer en sources esthétiques d'éclairage indirect à l'instar de tous ceux qui sont grillagés et qui filtrent la lumière ou de toute ouverture dans la maison, et ce, quelle que soit sa taille.

ALLE BAUELEMENTE haben einen Effekt auf das Licht. Massive verhindern seinen Durchgang und Durchsichtige lassen es frei passieren. Einige kann man in attraktive indirekte Lichtquellen verwandeln, angefangen bei Gittern, die das Licht durch seine Öffnungen sehen lassen, zu jeglicher anderen Öffnung im Gebäude, die Grösse spielt keine Rolle.

ONE WAY to make the outside of a building look superb is by building the outside wall in the form of a grid made of translucent natural stone blocks. The veining of each block needs to be studied so they can all be placed strategically to create an appealing pattern with a personal touch, which is then lit up from behind.

UNA ALTERNATIVA de la decoración exterior que deriva en una fachada soberbia consiste en construir el muro de acceso como una cuadrícula conformada por bloques de piedra natural translúcida. Conviene estudiar el veteado de cada módulo para colocarlo estratégicamente hasta lograr un dibujo interesante y con un toque personal, que se ilumina por la parte posterior.

SI L'ON DISPOSE d'une façade exceptionnelle, on peut décider de bâtir le mur entourant la porte principale avec des blocs de pierre translucide à l'état brut. Il faut toutefois préalablement bien étudier les veines naturelles du minéral pour créer ensuite un motif à la fois intéressant et personnalisé. Rétro-éclairé, les effets produits n'en seront que plus éclatants.

EINE MÖGLICHKEIT IM Design des Aussenbereiches, die zu einer unübertrefflichen Fassade führt, ist es die Mauer des Eingangsbereiches wie ein Mosaik, aus quadratischen lichtdurchlässigen Natursteinen zu konstruieren. Man sollte die Steine gemäss ihrer Maserung strategisch so anbringen, dass sie zusammen eine interessante Zeichnung mit einer persönlichen Note ergeben, die von hinten beleuchtet wird.

architecture arquitectónicos architectoniques architekten

3 *architectural and interior design project:* ABAX, fernando de haro, jesús fernández, omar fuentes y bertha figueroa

4-5 *architectural project:* GA GRUPO ARQUITECTURA, daniel álvarez fernández, *contributors:* pilar medina, rosa lópez, susana lópez, raúl chávez, sergio valdés, francisco puente y manuel campos

8 *interior design project:* ARCO ARQUITECTURA CONTEMPORÁNEA, josé lew y bernardo lew, *contributors:* oscar sarabia, jonathan herrejón, miguel ocampo, yuritza gonzález, itzel ortiz, nahela hinojosa, gabriela pineda, guillermo martínez, federico teista, martha tenopala y beatriz canuto

9 *interior design project:* MARTÍNEZ&SORDO, juan salvador martínez y luis martín sordo, *architectural project:* javier muñoz menéndez, *contributors:* pilar peñalver clemente, adela rodríguez ramírez y antonio martínez pérez

10 (left) *architectural project:* LASSALA + ELENES, carlos lassala m., eduardo lassala m., diego mora d., guillermo r. orozco y o.

11 (left) *architectural project:* GA GRUPO ARQUITECTURA, daniel álvarez fernández, *contributors:* pilar medina, rosa lópez, susana lópez, raúl chávez, sergio valdés, francisco puente y manuel campos

17 *interior design project:* TEXTURA®, walter allen, *architectural project:* jacobo gudiño, *contributors:* paolo rindone

18 (right) *architectural project:* guillermo trujillo vázquez, *interior design project:* nuria Lozano de hernández

19 *interior design project:* ECLÉCTICA DISEÑO, mónica hernández sadurní, *architectural project:* enrique muller y pablo díaz conde

20 *architectural project:* NOGAL ARQUITECTOS, josé m. nogal moragues

22 (top) *architectural and interior design project:* CONCEPTO RESIDENCIAL, josé manuel ruíz falcón,3 (bottom) *architectural project:* MUÑOZ ARQUITECTOS ASOCIADOS, javier muñoz menéndez, *contributors:* gareth lowe negrón

23 *architectural and interior design project:* enrique martorell gutiérrez, *contributors:* alejandro de noriega d´hyver de las deses y manuel cervantes

24-25 *architectural project:* JUAN CARLOS AVILÉS ARQUITECTOS, juan carlos avilés iguiniz

32 *architectural project:* ARTECK, francisco guzmán giraud, *interior design project:* TORBELI, elena talavera

40-41 *architectural and interior design project:* ABAX, fernando de haro, jesús fernández, omar fuentes y bertha figueroa

43 (top) *architectural project:* ARTECK, francisco guzmán giraud, (bottom) *architectural and interior design project:* ABAX, fernando de haro, jesús fernández, omar fuentes y bertha figueroa

44-45*architectural and interior design project:* ABAX, fernando de haro, jesús fernández, omar fuentes y bertha figueroa

46 *architectural project:* CENTRAL DE ARQUITECTURA, josé sánchez y moisés isón, *interior design project:* moisés isón, *contributors:* alejandro juárez herrera, nicolás vázquez herrmann y carlos del monte bergés

47 *architectural project:* CENTRAL DE ARQUITECTURA, josé sánchez y moisés isón, *interior design project:* simón hamui, *contributors:* crimson pasquinel, augusto fernández, socorro leyva y david bravo

58-59 *architectural and interior design project:* ABAX, fernando de haro, jesús fernández, omar fuentes y bertha figueroa

64-65 *interior design project:* MARQCÓ, covadonga hernández, *architectural project:* CARRANZA Y RUIZ ARQUITECTOS, alex carranza v. y gerardo ruiz díaz, *contributor:* mónica saucedo castillo

69 *architectural project:* MUÑOZ ARQUITECTOS ASOCIADOS, javier muñoz menéndez, *contributors:* gareth lowe negrón, andrea dutton ruiz, isabella rincon milet y luis miguel acuña gonzález

72-73 *architectural project:* LASSALA + ELENES, carlos lassala m., eduardo lassala m., diego mora d., guillermo r. orozco y o.

79 *architectural and interior design project:* ABAX, fernando de haro, jesús fernández, omar fuentes y bertha figueroa

80-81 *interior design project:* TEXTURA®, walter allen, *architectural project:* jacobo gudiño, *contributors:* paolo rindone

84 (right) *architectural project and construction:* ARCO ARQUITECTURA CONTEMPORÁNEA, josé lew y bernardo lew, *contributors:* olga berezhnaya, gina escorza, héctor garcía, federico teista, guillermo martínez, pedro feldman, gilberto prado, silvia guillen y beatriz canuto

85 *interior design project:* TERRÉS, javier valenzuela, fernando valenzuela y guillermo valenzuela, *architectural project:* francisco guzmán giraud

87 *architectural and interior design project:* ABAX, fernando de haro, jesús fernández, omar fuentes y bertha figueroa

92-93 *architectural project and construction:* ARCO ARQUITECTURA CONTEMPORÁNEA, josé lew y bernardo lew, *contributors:* olga berezhnaya, federico teista, leslye gonzález, guillermo martínez, pedro feldman, gilberto prado y beatriz canuto

95 *architectural project:* PRODE VIVIENDA, emilio ocejo

116 *architectural project:* ARQEE, jorge escalante pizarro, pedro escobar f.v. y jorge carral dávila

122-123 *architectural and interior design project:* ABAX, fernando de haro, jesús fernández, omar fuentes y bertha figueroa

128 (left) *architectural and interior design project:* ARQUITECTOS INTERIORES, SCP, mauricio ramírez pizarro y guadalupe ávila mendez, *contributors:* fabiola solis guillermo

130-131 *architectural and interior design project:* ABAX, fernando de haro, jesús fernández, omar fuentes y bertha figueroa

132-133 *architectural project:* GRUPO LBC, alfonso lópez baz, javier calleja y eduardo hernández, *interior design project:* geoffrey bradfield inc. ny

134 *architectural project:* LASSALA + ELENES, carlos lassala m., eduardo lassala m., diego mora d., guillermo r. orozco y o.

135 *architectural project:* GA GRUPO ARQUITECTURA, daniel álvarez fernández

138 *architectural and interior design project:* ABAX, fernando de haro, jesús fernández, omar fuentes y bertha figueroa

143 *architectural and interior design project:* ABAX, fernando de haro, jesús fernández, omar fuentes y bertha figueroa

144 (top) *architectural project:* GA GRUPO ARQUITECTURA, daniel álvarez fernández, *contributors:* pilar medina, rosa lópez, susana lópez, raúl chávez, sergio valdés, francisco puente y manuel campos, (bottom) *architectural project:* GGAD, gerardo garcía I.

147 *architectural project:* CARRANZA Y RUIZ ARQUITECTOS, alex carranza v. y gerardo ruiz díaz

148-149 *architectural project:* DI VECE Y ASOCIADOS, paolino di vece roux, *contributors:* edgar benítez, enrique reynoso, miguel sánchez.

151 *architectural and interior design project:* GGAD, gerardo garcía I.

161 *architectural and interior design project:* ABAX, fernando de haro, jesús fernández, omar fuentes y bertha figueroa

architecture arquitectónicos architectoniques architekten

230-231 *architectural project:* CENTRAL DE ARQUITFCTURA, josé sánchez y moisés isón, *interior design project:* simón hamui, *contributors:* crimson pasquinel, augusto fernández, socorro leyva y david bravo

232-233 *interior design project:* DUPUIS, alejandra prieto, cecilia prieto y claudia ortega

235 *interior design project:* COVILHA, blanca gonzález, maribel gonzález y meli gonzález

238-239 *architectural project:* CORNISH ARQUITECTOS, jorge cornish álvarez

240-243 *architectural project:* CARRANZA Y RUIZ ARQUITECTOS, alex carranza v. y gerardo ruiz díaz

244-245 *architectural and interior design project:* ELIZONDO ARQUITECTOS, renata r. elizondo

246 *architectural project:* CIBRIAN ARQUITECTOS, fernando cibrian castro

248-249 *architectural project:* CENTRAL DE ARQUITECTURA, josé sánchez y moisés isón, *interior design project:* moisés isón, *contributors:* alejandro juárez herrera, nicolás vázquez herrmann y carlos del monte bergés

250-251 *architectural project:* CIBRIAN ARQUITECTOS, fernando cibrian castro

252-253 *architectural and interior design project:* GGAD, gerardo garcía l.

254-255 *architectural project:* URBANISMO PAISAJE ARQUITECTURA, iñaki echeverria, *contributors:* eduardo álvarez, fernanda herrera, paola suárez, alfonso molina, maite echeverria, alejandro fernaández, patricio rubio, paul cremoux, josé carlos de silva, carlos luna, eliud aguirre, héctor gaitán

257 *architectural project:* CIBRIAN ARQUITECTOS, fernando cibrian castro

photography   fotográficos   photographiques   fotografen

alfonso de bejar - pg. 19

arturo chávez - pgs. 204-205, 232-233

© beta-plus publishing - pgs. 10 (right), 11 (right), 14-15, 18 (left), 21, 26-31, 34-38, 48-56, 62-63, 66-68, 70-71, 74-76, 84 (left), 89-91, 96-114, 117-120, 124-127, 128 (top right and bottom), 137, 140-141, 152-159, 164-165, 169-173, 178, 182, 184-191, 194-197, 203 (top), 236-237

carlos díaz corona - pgs. 148-49

carlos soto - pgs. 17, 80-81, 162

fabiola menchelli - pg. 200

fernando guerra - pg. 226

francisco quezada - pgs. 177, 180-181

héctor flora - pgs. 17, 80-81, 162

héctor velasco facio - pgs. 22 (top), 24-25, 32, 64-65, 132-133, 144 (bottom), 147, 151, 163, 211, 212-213, 235, 240-243, 246, 252-253, 257

jaime navarro - pgs. 8, 84 (right), 92-93

jordí farre - pg. 116

jorge cornish - pgs. 229, 238-239

jorge silva - pg. 23

jorge taboada - pgs. 244-245

josé gonzález - pgs. 163, 250-251

juan josé díaz infante - pg. 32

luis gordoa - pgs. 4-5, 11 (left), 144 (top), 166-167, 206-207,

marcos garcía - pgs. 10 (left), 72-73, 134, 174-175

maría fernanda olivieri san giacomo - pg. 95

maricarmen villanueva - pgs. 43 (top)

mark callanan - pgs. 3, 40-41, 43 (bottom), 44-45, 58-59, 79, 87, 122-123, 130-131, 138, 143, 161, 208, 222-223

mike paz y puente - pg. 9

mito covarrubias - pgs. 214-215, 221

nancy ambe - pgs. 17, 80-81, 162

olimpic kitchen and furniture collection - pgs. 198, 203 (bottom)

paul czitrom - pgs. 46-47, 135, 224-225, 230-231, 248-249

rafael gamo - pgs. 254-255

rene alvarado - pg. 128 (left)

roberto cárdenas cabello - pgs. 22 (bottom), 220

rolando córdoba - pg. 69

verónica areli martínez paz - pgs. 85, 201, 218-219

víctor benítez - pg. 20

Editado en Junio 2010. Impreso en China. El cuidado de
esta edición estuvo a cargo de AM Editores, S.A. de C.V.
Edited in June 2010. Printed in China. Published by
AM Editores, S.A. de C.V.